Praise for *The Leap*

A must-read for job seekers! Robert Dickie lays out a cutting edge yet practical game plan for everyone jumping into a job search.

KATIE KING, business development executive, Grant Thornton LLP and 20-year veteran to the staffing industry

Robert is one of the most thoughtful and genuine leaders I know, and the power and effectiveness of his advice, anecdotes, and action plans is evidenced in his success in applying them to his own life. My only regret is that I didn't have such a powerful "how-to" guide at my disposal earlier in my own career!

BRETT R. KEITH, managing partner, Rockwood Equity Partners LLC

Robert Dickie encourages us to take the next step in our working life with an accountable mentor, proven principles, and biblical wisdom. This book shows how a person can use a strong work ethic and apply it to the real world we live in now. How we work today really matters, and this book gives us the courage to jump and the knowledge to land safely.

DR. WILLIAM SHIELL, First Baptist Church of Tallahassee

A must-read! Robert shares very useful insights and direction for the large and increasing numbers who are, or soon will be, confronting career changes necessitated by our rapidly changing global economy impacting every facet of life.

ROD DAMMEYER, former partner, Arthur Anderson and CEO of Itel Corporation, current CEO of CAC

By combining godly wisdom from his experiences and those of some truly great men and women, Robert provides a solid framework for young professionals to process the otherwise bewildering choices around education, profession, and life itself.

HENRY KAESTNER, executive chairman, Bandwidth.com, managing partner, Sovereign's Capital

The Leap will help those at the beginning of their journey and also serves as a check-up for those of us already moving down life's path. I recommend this to all who want to "walk the walk" more than they want to "talk the talk."

RON SIMMONS, state representative Texas House District 65, chairman, Retirement Advisors of America, and vice chairman, Autism Society of America

Robert speaks in my Innovation & Social Media class at Lee University about the importance of personal branding. He is a very engaging speaker and brings real, actionable advice that can immediately impact anyone's future job prospects. Robert comes with a wealth of knowledge on the current job market and shares his wisdom freely. My students love hearing him speak. I look forward to utilizing his book as a resource in the classroom.

JARED POWERS, adjunct professor, Lee University Department of Communication Arts

This book is full of real life examples, practical application, and inspiration for every age group. I see glimpses of my husband Larry Burkett's teachings woven throughout each chapter and know that he would have been pleased to see Robert passionately following in his footsteps to help others. I am proud that Robert is carrying on his legacy through his writing and with his work at Crown.

JUDY BURKETT, cofounder of Christian Financial Concepts

In *The Leap*, Robert Dickie has nailed it—he's provided a resource that can help anyone in the marketplace find *both* firm footing *and* a realistic, optimistic perspective on their career. This is no academic summary, either—Robert walks the talk personally and professionally and provides proven, rock solid guidance.

CHRIS HERSCHEND, vice chairman, Herschend Family Entertainment

Experience, integrity, and insight are interwoven throughout Bob's work, life, and book, *The Leap*, which will give those ready to take a chance on a life "immeasurably more than they can ask or imagine." By picking up a book, most readers hope to enjoy the material and learn something. You'll get all that and more in Bob's insightful book that also provides practical steps for people ready to begin their next adventure.

KRISTI STONE HAMRICK, columnist, speaker, president, KSH Media, Inc.

The world has undergone some dramatic changes since the advent of the Internet. The way we live and work will continue to evolve as the remaining two-thirds of the world's population come online. Scary? Daunting? Confusing? Perhaps a little, but with Robert Dickie's book *The Leap* you will gain valuable insights into how to seek out the opportunities and derive value from this increasingly connected world.

NIKKI PARKER, regional director, Freelancer.com

People who are highly skilled at identifying problems are everywhere in our culture. "Don't blame the messenger," is their laid-back attitude. They stay on the sidelines waiting for someone else to take the leap and actually do something. Robert Dickie is a member of that rare fraternity of doers and this book is another example. I can't think of a better primer for the child/grandchild/intern/recent-hire about to tackle the world or for a mid-career person who needs a "between-the-ears" check-up. Blame the messenger? No. Congratulate this messenger and his timeless message.

LIEUTENANT COLONEL GARY GIBBS, United States Air Force (Ret)

Whether you are early on in your adult life and career or find yourself at a crossroads, *The Leap* will give you tangible takeaways that you can start implementing today to create quick but lasting positive results. This book is a practical application manual for the positive values that Bob Dickie has established for himself as a father, friend, military officer, business leader, and man of faith.

NEWTON B. COLLINSON IV, former president, Collinson Media & Events, entrepreneur

THE LEAP

Launching Your **FULL-TIME CAREER**
in Our **PART-TIME ECONOMY**

ROBERT DICKIE III

MOODY PUBLISHERS

CHICAGO

All Scripture quotations, unless otherwise indicated, are taken from the Holy
Bible, New International Version®, NIV®. Copyright © 1973, 1978, 1984, 2011
by Biblica, Inc.™ Used by permission of Zondervan. All rights reserved worldwide. www.zondervan.com. The "NIV" and "New International Version" are
trademarks registered in the United States Patent and Trademark Office by
Biblica, Inc.™

Scripture quotations marked NASB are taken from the *New American Standard
Bible*®, Copyright © 1960, 1962, 1963, 1968, 1971, 1972, 1973, 1975, 1977, 1995
by The Lockman Foundation. Used by permission. (www.Lockman.org)

Edited by Bailey Utecht
Cover Design: Connie Gabbert Design and Illustration
Interior Design: Smartt Guys design
Cover image of man on diving board copyright © by Bruce Wheadon/
        Shutterstock 698604. All rights reserved.
Author photo: John Black Photography

ISBN: 978-0-8024-1260-7

We hope you enjoy this book from Moody Publishers. Our goal is to
provide high-quality, thought-provoking books and products that connect
truth to your real needs and challenges. For more information on other books
and products written and produced from a biblical perspective, go to
www.moodypublishers.com or write to:

Moody Publishers
820 N. LaSalle Boulevard
Chicago, IL 60610

1 3 5 7 9 10 8 6 4 2

Printed in the United States of America

DEDICATION

I would like to dedicate this book to my amazing children, Lachlan, Trista, London, Amaris, and Charlize. You have been my inspiration for leaping because I've always wanted to provide the very best for all of you. Thank you for trusting me with each of your first real leaps into my arms from the side of a pool and know that I will always be there for you as you take your future proverbial "leaps" in life.

CONTENTS

CHAPTER 1

A LEAP IN THE MIDST OF A BLACK SWAN

"Courage is being scared to death and saddling up anyway."
—JOHN WAYNE

I've always done some of my best thinking on late-night flights. The military afforded me the opportunity to travel all around the world. Although each location is very different once you set foot on the ground, the world has a quiet peace as you fly high above it at night and watch the lights of the cities below you. It is a utopian view of a world without borders, issues, and problems. I have always thought those cityscapes at night are some of the most beautiful scenes. As I fly over neighborhoods and cities, I often think about the families below and their stories, hopes, dreams, and challenges. Everyone has unique challenges they are facing. During one particular flight from Milwaukee to Flint, Michigan, on a night in October of 2009, I started thinking about the recent and crippling economic collapse and the pain most households were going through below me. The Great Recession was in full effect. Our society was struggling and calling Americans to rise up—there was a global shift taking place, even as I flew over the Midwest landscape. There were businessmen and women leaving their safe and secure jobs to branch out on their own—pursuing new careers, creating start-ups, and buying out struggling companies. The writing was on the wall for me, but I was afraid.

OUR BLACK SWAN EVENT

The Great Recession marked something we call a Black Swan event, which in this case is the employment shift that began in 2007 and continues today. Black Swan events mark unpredictable, game-changing shifts that forever alter the course of what comes next. In retrospect, observers can see the event was bound to happen. They are like the proverbial meteor striking Earth, changing life as we know it. This Black Swan caused a new direction for job creation we are only beginning to address.

For aspiring workers, the strike of the economic collapse permanently altered their dreams for their bright future careers, and the repercussions remain severe. Today, as more Americans struggle to build a full-time life in a part-time world, the economic shift in job creation from steady employment to a patchwork of professions leaves many wondering when this will end. The *Washington Times* recently reported that 77 percent of the jobs created in 2013 were part-time.[1] Very little attention is being paid to how the historically low labor-participation rate is impacting evolving economic systems. Many assume the drastic shift to part-time job creation is an aftereffect of the crash that will slowly dissipate as the economy improves and we will resume the normal full-time employment we experienced in the past. I don't believe this is true. (See the chart on the next page.)

There are currently over 200 million people worldwide who are officially unemployed, with the unofficial number being much larger. Of that number, 75 million are under the age of 25.[2] Nation states are alarmed at the growing unemployment of the world's

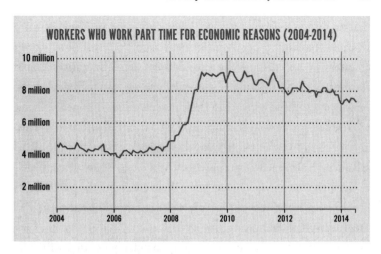

Source: Bureau of Labor Statistics (http://data.bls.gov/timeseries/LNS12032194)
Adapted from Alyson Hurt/NPR (www.npr.org/blogs/money/2011/09/13/140432433/-49-445)

youth and the potential destabilizing impact this could bring. This problem continues to grow daily, but unemployment is not the only issue—it is the lack of full-time jobs being created, and thus more and more of the global population need to patch together multiple jobs, freelance work, or "gigs" to make a living. This part-time workforce continues to grow. For example, a staggering 47 percent of the workforce in the UK is part-time.[3]

Three issues in particular are evidence of a Black Swan event reworking our economic structure: the increasing rate of globalization, the technological revolution displacing workforces, and the unbalanced laws and regulations governing free-market capitalism.

Today, globalization swallows up industries across national lines as businesses seek economies of scale to keep costs low and stockholder returns high. Even China is now losing jobs to other countries offering cheaper labor.

Outsourcing in search of cheap labor continues to displace more workers than any other event in the economy. In the proceeding chapters we will discuss the huge opportunities that are available for those who are seeking advanced education and technical skills. However, for those who are in the blue-collar jobs, I hope this book will be the proverbial "canary in the coal mine" and that we are able to sound the alarm to take action, seek more education and advanced training, and prepare for the shifts that are already well underway. Everyone needs to make these adjustments, but those in the manual-labor, less-skilled marketplace should be sprinting in the direction of change.

The second strike for such company-driven communities is how technological advances are also making large workforces irrelevant. If your job can be automated, it will be automated. It is just a matter of time. Bill Gates commented, "Technology over time will reduce demand for jobs, particularly at the lower end of the skill set . . . 20 years from now, labor demand for lots of skill sets will be substantially lower. I don't think people have that in their mental model yet."[4] This will create instability in regions all around the globe as workforces are displaced and left behind unable to find work in the new technologically advanced global market. In a recent *USA Today* article John Shinal wrote, "Workers wanting secure employment in coming decades will need skills that complement software applications rather than compete with them."[5] Career fields that will be hard to automate are ones that will rely on people skills, relationships, creativity, ones that leverage emotional intelligence, and ones where interpersonal activity is critical for success.

THE JOB MARKET MAY BE SUFFERING, BUT FOR THOSE WHO ARE PREPARED AND HAVE THE RIGHT SKILLS, THERE IS GREAT OPPORTUNITY.

However, the "knowledge economy" (jobs that require advanced education and skills) will grow leaps and bounds in the coming decade, and people with the right skills and education will be in high demand. As an example, a recruiter recently told me the unemployment rate in Nashville for anyone with a programming background is under 0.3 percent. She said, "They know how much they are worth and everyone needs them and they walk around town with a newfound arrogance because they can get anything they request." Another placement expert said, "It's crazy. I am placing C-students in programming who have just graduated, and they are getting six figure salaries. There just aren't enough of them." The job market may be suffering, but for those who are prepared and have the right skills, there is great opportunity.

Now you may be questioning your ability to program or fear you can't afford to go back to school and not know how you can take advantage of these opportunities. In the coming chapters I will highlight multiple online resources that will teach you programming and multiple technical disciplines that you can leverage today in your job and that will help you prepare for the future.

Finally, government initiatives that are supposed to improve our economy may actually cause harm to employees and the unemployed. A prime example of this is the new Affordable Care Act in the United States. The trickle-down impact of this new regulation on the economy is forcing business leaders to alter their workforce and the way their companies operate. One industry executive said, "[The ACA] is an impossible topic to be educated on. It changes weekly. We all know it makes it more expensive to hire employees, and since businesses have no idea what they are signing up for and what the cost is going to be, we aren't hiring. Actually, we are moving all our hiring to temp agencies so we can remain flexible." Joe Saad, CEO and founder of the placement firm Diag Partners in Michigan, said the last three years have been ones of explosive growth. "Companies in the past used firms like ours to outsource their recruiting. Now they are using us because they need help, but they can't afford to hire full-time employees, so they are looking for part-time and temp employees. We will continue to grow at record pace for the foreseeable future," opined Joe. When pressed further, most every business executive said the ACA in some way was impacting their hiring. This is just one example of how a regulation passed in Washington can have negative impacts in neighborhoods around the country.

In light of the three trends previously mentioned causing tectonic shifts in the global economy, what should we do? I believe we need to understand the new realities of the developing economy and the educational requirements needed to be successful. Furthermore, we need to be externally focused helping those in transition. Finally we need to prepare to take a leap in our career. From young to old one thing is certain, everyone is going to be in a state of transition in the coming years and those who have prepared for it will be best suited to navigate it successfully.

MY LEAP

So as my flight approached its destination city and I felt overwhelmed by this staggering shift facing our American economy, I contemplated another shift that would need to happen for the current workforce and the unemployed, for the next generation of workers, and for myself in order to have the fulfilling and successful careers people dream about. In the "old days," a college graduate would usually be able to secure a job with ease right out of school and possibly have the opportunity to stay in that company and keep advancing until retirement. This old way of being able to almost stumble into a lifelong career is no more. If you want to succeed in this new economy, it's going to require a leap of faith. I was ready to jump.

I left the military in 2004 to become the CEO of a small Midwest company back in my hometown of Grand Blanc, Michigan. Over the next five years the company experienced record growth, and we launched many new initiatives. I was fortunate to work with some very talented people and was blessed to be able to bring in a number of leaders from the military to help round out the team. We worked hard, played hard, and I enjoyed my time learning from each one of them. However, as key programs I was brought in to launch were winding down, I felt the burning desire to do something new. I felt stagnant, so I sought advice from a number of mentors regarding what I should do. There were a few different perspectives, and some said, "Bob, we are in the worst recession of our lifetime. You are married with four kids. Setting out to launch your own thing right now seems nuts." But my advisors, which included my Young Presidents' Organization (YPO) forum mates in Detroit and a host of entrepreneurs who themselves had made similar leaps in their careers, encouraged me to follow my heart and make the leap. I was fascinated with technology and wanted to launch an application company with some partners. I wanted to start a consulting business, leveraging the things I had learned in the military and my time in the business world, and work with other companies on new challenges. I wanted to pursue advanced education, and I desperately wanted to move from Michigan to the warmer South to raise our family.

To do this would require me to take a huge leap of faith. As I flew home that night, I prepared my talking points for a phone call I would have with the owner and chairman of the board the next morning regarding my intent to resign and pursue a new career direction. I wrote up my official letter of resignation for the rest of the board and mentally prepared to take the leap. As the plane touched down that night at Bishop Airport in Flint, I remember a complete peace that came over me regarding the decision. I knew it would not be easy, but I was excited to be embarking on a new journey and following my passions. That Monday morning I made the phone call with the chairman, spoke with the rest of the board, and began to prepare the transition plan. The following days and weeks were a whirlwind of activity. I had crossed the Rubicon and there was no going back.

Taking the leap is scary and often painful, so I certainly don't want to romanticize my decision or transition. Looking back, it is easy to remember all the victories and harder to remember the challenges I faced along the way. When taking a leap, I have learned that you have to be flexible and be ready to change directions on short notice. It took us much longer to sell our home in Michigan than we anticipated, but we were finally able to relocate back to Knoxville, Tennessee, where my wife and I had met, gotten married, and started our family. The road to launching my consulting practice and technology company presented multiple challenges I had not anticipated.

THIS IS NOT OUR GRANDFATHERS' ECONOMY, AND THERE ARE NEW RULES EVERYONE NEEDS TO UNDERSTAND.

Mainly, it took longer than I expected. But it also offered valuable learning experiences and opportunities I never dreamed I would have. I was able to work with some great companies in multiple industries, opportunities like a Google Venture start-up, non-profits, and companies in the direct sales industry.

As my partners and I continued to press forward with our technology initiatives, I continued to work as a consultant. My good friend Ron Simmons, chairman and founder of Retirement Advisors of America (RAA) in Dallas, was having breakfast with a friend in Dallas and passed my name on to him when he heard that he needed some help with some initiatives he was undertaking. And so my relationship with Chuck Bentley, CEO of Crown, was born. After meeting with him in Atlanta to discuss his plans for the future, I accepted an offer to come on as a part-time consultant in January 2011 to help in a corporate transition. A few months later, Chuck and the board presented an offer to come on full-time as the president of Crown. This was a perfect opportunity for me to merge the things I was passionate about in the business world with the things I was passionate about regarding non-profit work and serving those in need. When I took that leap in October of 2009, I had no idea of the twists and turns I would take over the coming years. Many times I have heard the quote, "Man makes plans and God laughs," and I know for certain God was guiding my steps. I could look behind me and see in my career how God had opened doors and prepared me for the challenges and opportunities He was placing in front of me. During this same time I received an email from Harvard Business School accepting my application for an executive course, and I started the Harvard Business School Executive Program for YPO presidents. All the dreams and goals I had hoped for as I sat on that Delta flight in 2009, preparing to take the leap and resigning from my safe job to launch out on my own and follow my passions, had come to pass.

I was fortunate to have mentors around me who helped me analyze the opportunities and landscape and provided wise counsel and encouragement when I needed it most. I don't advocate taking the leap without a plan. Those who stand on the sidelines of life waiting for something good to happen will grow old waiting and watching everyone around them taking deliberate and intentional action and #winning in the game of life.

This book is a tool for you. I want you to understand how to craft a plan for your life and career that's in alignment with your strengths and values, how to avoid anchors that can hold you back, how to take the leap and accomplish your plan, and why taking the leap matters. The global economy is changing all around us. The Black Swan at the start of the Great Recession has changed the paradigm of work, jobs, and careers. What happened and what this means for the global workforce is still being discovered, but one thing is for sure: this is not our grandfathers' economy, and there are new rules everyone needs to understand. Understanding these changes is important. Developing a plan and taking action is critical.

LEAPING BY EXAMPLE

A LEAP OF FAITH: Tom Darden, *Cherokee Investment Partners founder and CEO*

By any measure Tom Darden—founder and CEO of Cherokee, the $2 billion private equity firm investing in brownfield redevelopments—is a success story worth studying. With a bachelor's and master's degree from the University of North Carolina and a law degree from Yale, Tom has an educational pedigree anyone would admire. Tom made his leap following graduation from Yale while he was working with the prestigious consulting firm Bain & Company. It was a safe and secure job at a prestigious firm, but Tom wanted to do something different. He was aware of Cherokee Sanford Group, the struggling North Carolina company on the verge of going out of business. Tom pulled together a plan to purchase the company and see if he could turn it around. "It was such a disaster when I bought it. It was going to fail without me, and if it failed at least I knew I had tried. I could always go back to practicing law," said Tom. "I was a good saver and had saved up at least a year of savings before I made the move." The move proved to be a pivotal moment in his career as he turned around the company, which became the largest privately held brick manufacturer in the United States. This gave birth to Cherokee Investment Partners, the private equity firm Tom leads today. It has massive impact around the world in environmental land reclamation.

Pressing Tom further to understand how he can take such big leaps and press through the fear that most people would have succumbed to, he said, "Bob, any fear I have faced has always been a function of failure or embarrassment, never about money. I also never let fear stop me from doing what is right. When facing those fears, I would initially be upset at myself for not having more faith. Faith is a big part of your journey. I have learned to have comfort in faith, not accomplishments." As I closed the interview and asked Tom what words of advice and counsel he would give people entering the workplace today, without pause he answered, "The central message I would convey is this: their own opinions of their current situation and the things that happen to them in their career are almost always going to be wrong. This is essential to understand. If something happens and you think it is good or bad, you really don't know. Many times you may perceive something to be bad, like if you get fired or lose your job, but in reality it is good for you because it launches you in a new direction. The inverse is also true. Never form an opinion about your current circumstances because your opinion will almost always be wrong." I asked him if he felt this changes over time and with experience, thinking I knew the answer. Again he surprised me. "Bob, you really don't. You have to take each situation as it comes and only time will tell if what happened is good or bad." Time has proven that Tom Darden is one of a kind. In 2010 he and his company were awarded the YPO Corporate Social Responsibility Award because of his work to return hazardous waste sites to productive use through environmental remediation. He currently has over 550 properties under management worldwide and his environmental work is making the world cleaner and safer for everyone. His leap is benefiting us all.

CHAPTER 2

MAKE
A PLAN

"Plans are only good intentions unless they immediately degenerate into hard work." —PETER DRUCKER

As an officer in the United States Air Force I often heard the phrase, "If you don't have a plan, you are planning to fail." This wise counsel is not only great advice for leaders preparing for combat operations, but it is also crucial for those in the job market today.

The reality is that without help, it can be hard to build a plan and then execute it. Having a plan of action can make stressful situations manageable with a specific step-by-step approach to reach your objectives. With a trusted mentor or advisor helping us it can be much easier, but it will still require time and thought to put it all down in a written document so we can reference it regularly and make sure that we are on track.

The new economy has affected all aspects of life, and the old rules no longer apply. To navigate the ever-changing economic landscape, it will be critical to start with a deliberate plan—a life plan, freedom fund, and early planning for retirement.

First of all, we need to know where we are and where we want to go. When you are orienteering in the woods, knowing your location is a critical first step to getting to your final destination. You might think, *I know where I am . . . I'm a student looking for a job*, or *I'm about to launch a new start-up company.* Unfortunately, this is not what we are talking about. We need to go deeper. Discovering who you are—your gifts, skill sets, desires, and values—will tell you where you are in life. This is your frame of reference. From there you can build a career plan that will maximize your talents and gifts to help you achieve a life of meaning and purpose.

DISCOVERING WHO YOU ARE—YOUR GIFTS, SKILL SETS, DESIRES, AND VALUES—WILL TELL YOU WHERE YOU ARE IN LIFE.

In this new economy it is critical that everyone have a high level of self-awareness to understand how they have been made, what their unique gifts and talents are, and what their passion and life goals are. In the past, high school and college were used as years of self-discovery, where people could take classes and over time decide on their career. Some even went on adventures in their 20s, continuing to live a Spartan college-existence, traveling and working multiple jobs that might have varied considerably with no thought to the future. It was easier to jump into a career path of choice.

Today is different. Mounting education costs are drowning graduates in debt. Spending more time in college taking classes and dragging out the experience is no longer ideal, as it only adds to the mounting student-loan debt a graduate carries. The average student is graduating today with $30,000 in student-loan debt and having a hard time finding a job in their career of choice.[1] Student-loan debt is now $1.2 trillion and is the second largest form of debt in America, behind mortgages and ahead of credit card debt.[2] Many economists believe the real-estate bubble that exploded in 2007 will be followed by a student-loan burst that is looming even now. This has led many to debate the value of education today. Some have argued that college educations are not worth it and are a waste of time. I spent the past year interviewing leaders from all over the world—economists, CEOs, placement-agency executives, and recruiters—and everyone agrees that education is critical for success in this new economy. Because this has been a hotly debated topic I want to highlight some key facts here. The goal is threefold:

1. Obtain useable knowledge you can leverage in your career.
2. Obtain the right certification or degree for your desired career path.
3. Do 1 and 2 as quickly and inexpensively as possible.

EDUCATION

In January of 2014, while attending the YPO Presidents' Program at Harvard Business School, I was able to have dinner with professor Krishna Palepu and his wife, Laurie. Krishna taught at Harvard for 29 years, 10 of those at HBS, and is currently the Senior Advisor to Harvard's president, so I jumped at the chance to ask him questions about the global economy and education. Knowing that Krishna and Laurie had children, one of my questions was, "What are the three most important things you could tell your children today to be ready to have success in this new economy?" Without pause Krishna said, "First, become a lifelong learner. Second, learn to speak a foreign language. Third, travel the world to get a global understanding of the different cultures and how people see and interact with the world." Understanding how technology was changing our world, I realized that all three were things that anyone could do right from their home. Yes, even if someone did not have the money to travel the world, they could spend time online to learn in-depth about countries, regions, and cultures of the entire globe. Technology was making it possible for everyone to have a world-class education at their fingertips.

In the first chapter I pointed to a number of sources that foretell of this new global economy becoming more and more dominated by technology, and those who have the advanced skills and training will disproportionately win in this economy. Those who do not have the requisite skill and training will find it extremely difficult to find quality work and gainful long-term employment. Based on these comments some might think, *I can't afford the time or money to go back to school to get more education.* Don't be discouraged. Today, anyone in the world can receive a world-class education for free, right at home, and I want to tell you how.

The amount of education you might need depends on your life plan and goals. For those who want to climb the corporate ladder and obtain leadership positions within Fortune 500 companies, college degrees and advanced degrees are going to be *very* important. The college you attend is equally important, as certain colleges with "prestigious brands" are seen differently than a small community college degree in these environments. There is no way around it. So if that is your desired career path, it is important to understand those dynamics. For those who aspire to be entrepreneurs and to start your own companies, the path can be a bit different. The goal: usable knowledge with the ability to execute in the marketplace; the degree or institution it is from is largely irrelevant to the entrepreneur. No matter where you are in your educational journey, I encourage you to grow as a lifelong learner and continue to advance your knowledge base and skill sets. Here is how you can start.

MOOCS – MASSIVE OPEN ONLINE COURSES

Massive Open Online Courses (MOOCs) are college- and graduate-level courses being taught over the web. A person can enroll in a class being taught on campus, use the same course curriculum, be taught by the same professor, and many times monitor the exact class being taught on campus via the web. Many of these courses come with a certificate of completion. The very best universities in the world like Harvard, Yale, MIT, Stanford, Penn, Duke, and

Michigan are now offering many of their classes via a MOOC environment, allowing everyone the ability to have a world-class education for free.

Over dinner, Krishna Palepu told me the story of when MIT launched a MOOC with one of its hardest courses taught at the school. Over 150,000 people around the world signed up to take the class. At the end of the class, one of the top scores came from a 15-year-old boy in Ulan Bator, the capital of Mongolia. He was awarded a full scholarship to MIT and started a year later full-time.

THE GOAL: USABLE KNOWLEDGE WITH THE ABILITY TO EXECUTE IN THE MARKETPLACE; THE DEGREE OR INSTITUTION IT IS FROM IS LARGELY IRRELEVANT TO THE ENTREPRENEUR.

I recommend visiting Coursera.org, which is an online aggregator of MOOC courses from the top colleges in the world. You can search for a program, see when it is starting, and see which ones offer a certificate of completion. List these courses and certificates of completion on your resume under the heading "Continuing Education." This shows that you are not satisfied with what you may have learned in the past but that you are challenging yourself, growing daily, and looking to the future.

LEARN TO CODE

As I have traveled the world I have heard many people mention that the global language of business is English. Some have said they think in the future it will be Chinese. Only time will tell. Regardless, many will tell you that in the coming years equally as important or more important than English will be the ability to code. Technology transcends all global boundaries, and those who can speak and understand "code" are in the driver's seat in this new economy. It is reported that over the next 10 years there will be 2 million unfilled technology jobs.[3] Companies are looking for MBAs who can assume leadership positions but can understand code, as this is becoming a new skill even leaders need. There is virtually zero unemployment in the coding field, with recruiters complaining they can't find enough talent for the open positions they need to fill. Those same coders can ask a king's ransom, and their demands are being met. If you want job security for the future, learn to code. Just like MOOCs there are many websites that will teach coding for free, from the basics all the way up to advanced coding, and will also provide certificates for completion. Here are my favorites:

1. Codecademy.com
2. Udacity.com
3. ReFactorU.com
4. KhanAcademy.com

Again, list any course you take and certificate of completion on your resume. Every department in every company today somehow interfaces with technology. Regardless of your background, if you start building your coding knowledge and certifications you will be quantum leaps ahead of your peers when interviewing for jobs.

PODCASTS

I don't know what I would do without my iPhone and the podcast content I have downloaded daily. I am amazed at the amount of educational material I can carry in my pocket and the amount of time I have to invest in my continuing education every day— from my commute, running, lunch breaks, and even shopping. I am always listening and taking notes. For aspiring entrepreneurs, I highly recommend the following podcasts, but my favorite by far is Stanford's *E-Corner*.

1. Stanford University's *E-Corner*, "Entrepreneurial Thought Leader" series
2. Harvard Business Review's *HBR IdeaCast*

3. *Chicago Booth Podcast*
4. London Business School's Official Podcast
5. *Seth Godin's Start-Up School*

ADVANCED EDUCATION

One of my favorite sites that I use regularly is KhanAcademy .com. No matter what subject matter you would like to learn, they have videos for you. It has been one of the most widely used global learning platforms, bringing world-class education to the masses. Since I am such a fan of this online learning environment, I am currently working with a team to launch CrownBiz.com/venture-academy-listing to bring Harvard Business School case studies to entrepreneurs. These are taught by an HBS graduate in a similar fashion to how HBS presents them. You might not have time for a two-year MBA, but many of the concepts and key principles taught in the HBS MBA-program can be learned online using the same case studies and teaching methods.

> EDUCATION FOR THE SAKE OF "DISCOVERING YOURSELF" OR TO FIND OUT WHICH CAREER IS BEST FOR YOU IS A LUXURY MANY CANNOT AFFORD TODAY.

I hope I have convinced you that education is important. For some, this will be a very beneficial option. However, education for the sake of "discovering yourself" or to find out which career is best for you is a luxury many cannot afford today. There are alternative ways to gain this experience and self-awareness.

KNOW YOURSELF

The Bible says that everyone is "fearfully and wonderfully made" (Psalm 139:14). You and I are totally different, and there will never be another person like us. God has given each of us special talents, skills, desires, and passions in His unique design for our lives. When we understand how we are hardwired and we pursue a career that is in total alignment with our skills, life is much easier. It is like we are swimming in a river with a powerful current that is helping us reach our destination. However, if we don't understand how we are made with our unique values and talents, we could find ourselves on a path of study or in a career where we are misaligned. Being misaligned is hard work, painful, and sometimes full of misery. If you know someone who is struggling in life and not happy with their job or course of study, it is possible they are misaligned in a key area of their life.

If you have never really been able to discover those talents or have always felt that you have been living outside of your God-given design, it is never too late to gain this self-awareness. I have seen so many people who were struggling and dissatisfied in life, but once they developed a great sense of self-awareness, their life was forever changed.

So how do we find out who we are so we can begin to build a life plan and start our journey? Over two decades ago the late Larry Burkett, founder of Crown, realized there was a need in the marketplace for an assessment to help people find their educational and career paths based on their unique talents, abilities, passions, and values. He saw people making major mistakes because they did not have a life plan. He assembled a top-notch group of professors and PhD candidates at the University of Georgia and set out to design a unique assessment to help people begin this process. After investing thousands of hours, millions of dollars, and multiple iterations, the online career-assessment software Career Direct was born. Over 250,000 people have used this assessment to help build a life plan.[4] This program is now run by Dr. Jan Strydom, and is available in twenty languages and in forty-nine countries. I highly recommend this service as the starting point to understand your skills, talents, values, and goals. Once you know these, you will better understand where you should invest your time in your coursework and in the workforce. You will live a life of purpose and meaning because you will be aligned with how you were made. Crown offers trained consultants who will walk you through this online assessment program, help you understand your results, and guide you in creating a life plan to reach your objectives so you can live a life of passion and fulfillment. To learn more about this assessment you can visit www.CareerDirect-ge.org.

When people understand themselves more deeply and have clarity on their unique talents and gifts, they can take the next step and start to craft a life plan. Every stage of life needs to have a life plan, and I have found that the people who are the most successful are ones who have written out goals and crafted a plan that they execute daily. I recommend creating a short-term and long-term plan, with goals along the way to measure progress. These goals will change over time, but the most important thing is to set a goal and start taking action to get there.

CRAFT A PLAN

For a young millennial graduating college, the goal may be to find a good first job, pay down college debt, map out a ten-year career track, and establish their *freedom fund*, which I will explain later. For a mid-career professional who is unhappy in their work and looking to transition to something more in alignment with their gifts, it might be to reduce debt, establish their freedom fund, and start networking and branding themselves with a goal to have new employment within one year. For those out of work looking to get back into the workforce, the goals may be to totally change the way you are networking and searching for work, to get a mentor to help you, and to polish up on some volunteer work and education to help make yourself the top candidate for your company of choice. Each person will have their own unique short- and long-term goals but the key is to write them down, have a few mentors who can help you and also hold you accountable, and then take action each day toward those goals.

There is nothing more powerful and encouraging than to

have a plan in place and to know you are making progress daily. Helplessness and discouragement come when we seem to be in a hopeless situation and each day is like the next. The classic movie *Groundhog Day* with Bill Murray illustrates this perfectly. Bill plays the role of a news anchorman who continues to wake up every morning reliving the same day of February in a cold, dreary town of Pennsylvania forced to cover the news story of the infamous groundhog Punxsutawney Phil. The nightmare of his existence continues day after day. Things finally change for Bill when he adjusts his attitude and approaches each day as if it were new. He learns new skills, makes friends, and helps those in need. His nightmare turns into a very charmed existence. The same is true for anyone who has a plan and takes action each day with a positive attitude.

> **THERE IS NOTHING MORE POWERFUL AND ENCOURAGING THAN TO HAVE A PLAN IN PLACE AND TO KNOW YOU ARE MAKING PROGRESS DAILY.**

The new economy has not only impacted the importance of a life plan and changed the way we have used the college years in the past for self-discovery, but it has also changed how we should prepare for our career. In the past there was a commonly held belief that all you had to do was graduate from college with good grades, get a great job with a major company, slowly move up the corporate ladder, and you would be set to retire with a gold watch and modest guaranteed pension. It was a simple plan but filled with fatal flaws that have slowly been exposed. This "45 year plan" started showing cracks decades ago. Major corporations (General Motors, Microsoft, Hewlett-Packard, IBM, Ford, Citigroup, etc.) that once seemed secure, offering "safe careers," have started laying off large portions of their workforce, while some have gone out of business completely (Enron, WorldCom, Washington Mutual, Lehman Brothers). As an aging population started retiring and drawing on their reserves, it was obvious the funding was not adequate for the promises that had been made. Corporations like General Motors

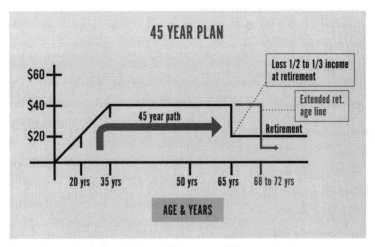

Adapted from The Team Vision (www.theteamvision.net/45-year-plan.html)

and even major cities like Detroit started negotiating with their workers to reduce pension benefits.

People started seeing that jobs at the "majors" were no longer a safe and a sure bet. Labor forces around the world feared layoffs and downsizing. For those who were laid off, it often took months and sometimes years to find new work. Unemployment benefits were quickly exhausted, leaving families with no income and little savings. As companies wanted to shed the burden of offering benefits, more and more part-time work has been created, leaving a growing part of the workforce in a continual state of uncertainty and fear.

SPENDING AND THE FREEDOM FUND

Graduating college seniors today are told they can expect to have eight to fourteen different jobs throughout their career. Those currently in the workforce are having to relocate and many times change jobs as well. This transition of the workforce is causing great strain on families who are not prepared. This is partly because the rules have changed and many are playing by the old rules.

In the old system, a new employee could hire in at one of these major companies with reasonable assurance that they would have a good-paying job for years to come. It was normal to take a risk and buy a home, put down roots, and start building a life. Over time, some took on more risk and instead of saving for retirement and having a large cash reserve for emergencies they would purchase a second vacation home with a boat. People rented vehicles, joined country clubs, and before long these people had a high monthly burn rate.

IN THE OLD SYSTEM, A NEW EMPLOYEE COULD HIRE IN AT A MAJOR COMPANY WITH REASONABLE ASSURANCE THAT THEY WOULD HAVE A GOOD-PAYING JOB FOR YEARS TO COME.

In the business world the term *burn rate* means negative cash flow. It is used to calculate the amount of money a business would need to spend each month to support operations. This is an important term to understand, as we will use it multiple times throughout the book. If a company had $100,000 in cash reserves (in a bank account) and had a fixed burn rate of $10,000 a month, assuming they were not generating any revenue or profit, they would be out of cash in 10 months.

Heading into the crash of 2008, it was normal for many American families to be in credit card debt and also have a large monthly burn rate. The average American family had more debt with their mortgages, car loans, student-loan debts, and credit cards than they had in savings and retirements, and thus they were considered "highly leveraged." Just as the banks and investment firms who were highly leveraged heading into the crisis went out of business, many families had to file for bankruptcy and many more struggled when their cash flow decreased or stopped completely. These types of events are not rare but rather more frequent in this new economy. So it is important to *not* be in debt, highly leveraged, and without a good cash reserve for emergencies. Although many have given advice to have a small cash reserve of $1,000 for emergencies, I believe all Americans should be working to have a liquid cash reserve equal to one year's burn rate, which is what I call a *freedom fund*.

I had a business associate when I was younger tell me he had built a fund that would allow him to walk away from his job at a moment's notice when he was finally fed up. He explained that it gave him a sense of security knowing that he could support his family without a job, and if things ever got bad enough at work he could just walk out and even say a few long-bottled-up, choice words to his boss as he left. I found it disturbing that each day was filled with such misery at his job that he had to create such a fund just to help him get through. His attitude and heart were obviously in the wrong place, but he was on to something. He realized that with this savings he was afforded greater flexibility than his coworkers who were living from paycheck to paycheck with no safety net.

In the current environment, many placement-firm executives have stated that for every $10,000 in salary, it takes one month to find a job. For example, a person looking to replace a $30,000-a-year job should expect it to take three months. I have known highly quali-fied friends with proven track records and stellar backgrounds who have been without work for over a year while they actively searched each day.

Those in the workforce today will most likely find themselves in a state of transition at some point in the future. The younger you are, the more times you will transition in your career. A chosen few might be able to move from one job to the next with no interruption. However, we are seeing many people who will have gaps in their employment where they may be out of work for months, and even longer. Because of this it is important to develop a freedom fund. I call it a freedom fund because its name denotes what it gives you. Once fully developed, you have a great sense of freedom and flexibility. It provides a sense of security for those times of uncertainty. It is 100 percent cash that you can get on a moment's notice. It is not equity tied up in your home, the perceived value in a car or boat that you can sell, stocks, bonds, or any other form of investment. To establish this we must work on two different things at once. First, we want to start reducing all unnecessary and wasteful

I HAVE NEVER PURCHASED ANYTHING IN LIFE THAT GAVE ME A GREATER FEELING THAN THAT OF HAVING MARGIN IN MY LIFE AND THE ABILITY TO HELP OTHERS.

expenses in our life. Second, we will look for ways to increase our income and add secondary sources of revenue. I will go more in depth on these two action steps in later chapters.

Regarding the reduction of spending, remember this critical point: depending on the economist you speak with, the American economy is driven between 40 and 70 percent by consumer spending.[5] We are bombarded every day with advertisements of all the newest technology, fashions, cars, homes, and lifestyle items that we supposedly need to purchase to make our lives "better." Sadly, it seems like today many people derive more of their self-worth from the brand of shoes they wear and the car they drive than from their character and integrity. I have never purchased anything in life that gave me a greater feeling than that of having margin in my life and the ability to help others.

As we reduce our monthly burn rate we will be increasing our margin. Margin is created when you have a higher income than your monthly burn rate. For example, if you make $2500 a month, and your monthly burn rate is $2000, you have a $500 monthly margin. Throughout this book we will talk about driving down our burn rate while looking for ways to increase our income, which will help increase our margin. The more margin we have the more we are able to help others, save, and prepare for retirement. We will talk more about this in the next chapter. For now it is important to start building your freedom fund and understand that to fully fund this you need to know your burn rate.

As you start running the calculations in your head you might be thinking, *Wow, my burn rate is high and I have no margin. How in the world can I build a freedom fund?* We will start to get into the specifics in the next chapter. The first step is to understand the information required to build it, understand why it is important to have the type of freedom and security it will give you and your family once you have it, and make it a written goal of yours to achieve.

Once you have your plans written down and you have a better understanding of where you are, your gifts and passions, and where you will have the greatest opportunity for success, you are closer to taking your leap. Understanding the importance of your freedom fund to your career and working to fully fund it is a critical next step as you work to avoid anchors that will weigh you down.

LEAPING BY EXAMPLE

MAKING A PLAN: Josh Linkner, cofounder and CEO of Detroit Venture Partners, *New York Times* bestselling author

In 2009, as a serial entrepreneur and a four-time tech founder, Josh Linkner was ready to take his next leap. Josh was a Young Presidents' Organization member and a rising star as the founder of ePrize, the largest interactive promotion agency in the world. He was also about to author his first book, *Disciplined Dreaming*, which quickly became a *New York Times* bestseller. Josh decided to leave ePrize to help start Detroit Venture Partners. He became the CEO, raised over $150 million in capital to invest in over 100 businesses and wrote his second book, *The Road to Reinvention*, which again became a *New York Times* bestseller. Josh is humble, smart, and has a career of taking leaps and knowing how to stick the landing each time. One thing is certain: Josh knows how important planning is when you take the leap.

"In venture capital, it is very important to have a business plan. The most successful businesses are ones that build and execute great plans. Your career is no different. Having a plan is critical for success. Think of your plan as Google

Maps for your career. You have to know where you are and where your destination is, and then you can navigate your way. There are many possibilities, but you have to start with where you are and where you want to finish." Josh continued by saying, "Great plans need multiple checkpoints along the way. If you get off course or something changes, you will need to pivot and take an alternate route. Don't continue executing on a plan that is obviously not working. You have to regularly reevaluate the plan."

Josh learned four key lessons along his journey:

1. **Make your own plan.** "Don't do what others think you should do. How do you want to be remembered? This is much more important than your starting salary. Follow your calling."

2. **Take risks.** "Early in your career is the best time to take risks. Say there are two people with similar backgrounds and skill sets. After college, one goes out to start a company and the other goes to work for a big consulting agency. If the person who starts a company ends up failing, I believe they will still be further ahead than the consulting guy who is having success. The start-up guy will have real-world experience, have more knowledge of the market, and be more marketable for his next leap. The guy who played it safe and went to a top-consulting firm is just being taught how to think like everyone else. In my career I have found the start-up guy, in the long run, is much better off."

3. **Don't fear failure.** "We all have been socialized that failure is bad. It's not! That is when we learn. In Silicon Valley, failure is a badge of honor, not a scarlet letter. If you fail, learn from it, own it, and be able to explain to

people how you are better because of it. It makes you better in business and a better leader!"

4. **Craft plan B.** "People think you craft a plan B for when things go wrong. I think you should craft a plan B for when things go right. It is very important to know what you will do if and when you have success. Spend more time thinking about this than potential failures."

STICKING THE LANDING

- Think of three people you trust and have a personal relationship with who can provide counsel to you as you start to create a life plan.

- What are your talents and skills? Take a Career Direct® assessment with a trained consultant and review your 30-page report. Creating a plan that will leverage your abilities and skills has a much greater chance of success than chasing after a dream that is not in your gifting. www.CareerDirect.org

- Be intentional in starting to write a one-year, three-year, and five-year plan. Even if this changes over time, the act of going through this exercise is important. Start to dream about your future by writing down your goals.

- Write down a list of things you can do each day to take small steps toward your goals. Review these at the end of each week to stay focused on the long-term goal. Goals that are not focused on regularly will not be achieved. Likewise, goals with no daily action taken have a lower chance of success.

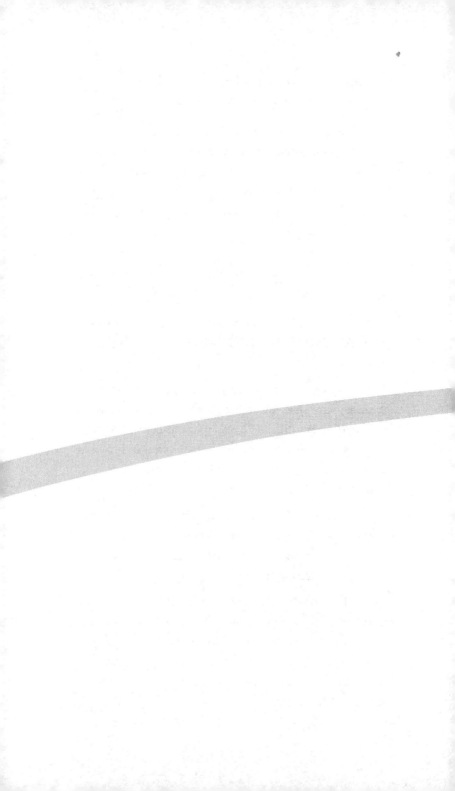

CHAPTER 3

AVOID ANCHORS

"A man in debt is so far a slave." —RALPH WALDO EMERSON

Many years ago I stood with an older colleague on the deck of his beautiful home. We talked about where he was in life, the challenges he was facing, and the stress piled on him that most people did not know about. He muttered a phrase that has stayed with me to this day. As the summer humidity stuck to us both, he looked out over the city and said, "Bob, you know how 'the mass of men lead lives of quiet desperation'? I think it's true. And no one ever knows about it." You could hear the hopelessness in his voice as he shared a rare moment of utter honesty. Amidst the heat, that comment somehow had a chilling effect on me, and it is something I have grown to better understand over the years. Here stood a man who had accomplished so much in life, had every sign of material and corporate success, a beautiful family, and the life that most people dream about.

Being a close friend and confidant, I knew he felt trapped. He was anchored in life, in a career that left him unfulfilled and always yearning for more, trapped by his material success and not even enjoying it. He was on a treadmill where the pace continued to increase, he was tired, and he could not jump off. It was easy to see he had all the wrong anchors in life.

There are good anchors in life, and we generally call them *foundations*. They are the things that will last, upon which we build our future. In the Bible, Jesus says to build your foundation on the rock and not on the sand. Good anchors are things like family, faith, and traditions that keep us grounded on our journey in life. We need to build and protect those anchors. However, there are negative anchors that hurt people as they start to build their careers, and those are ones we need to understand and navigate carefully. Especially in this economy, it is important to not be encumbered with anchors that will hold us back.

BUILDING A LIFE IN YOUR 20s AND 30s THAT ALLOWS YOU TO TRANSITION QUICKLY WILL HELP YOU HAVE SUCCESS FASTER THAN YOUR PEERS WHO ARE LOCKED INTO CERTAIN LOCATIONS.

Those coming out of college looking to land a job need to create a life that allows them to be flexible. Building a life in your 20s and 30s that allows you to transition quickly will help you have success faster than your peers who are locked into certain locations. The best opportunities might mean you have to move often in order to build a resume and skill set as you progress in your career. One thing is certain: the mosaic that you create that will comprise your career and entire life will look vastly different from your parents' and grandparents'.

The same flexibility is needed for the mid-career professionals and a new growing demographic, people over the age of 55 who are crafting a second career for the next stage in life. I have spoken with many seniors who once thought they would be able to retire, only to wake up one day and realize they would need to create a working retirement to handle the medical bills, diminished savings, and investments they once thought would be there for them in their later years. Just as it is important for someone young to create a life that allows them to be flexible to take advantage of opportunities, it is even more important for the older generation to create this flexibility and be willing to change to maximize opportunity. Many times it is more difficult for this segment of the population because families have developed, kids are established and in school, you have roots in an area, you have a mortgage, and people are comfortable with their routines. It is tough, but if you want to further your career and put yourself in the best position to provide for your family you need to consider how flexible you are. If you are fortunate, you get to decide whether you need to move. Many, however, based on circumstances, will be forced to move to new locations to have meaningful employment or opportunities.

The four most common anchors that I have come to see hinder people during these transitions are mental, financial, physical, and spiritual. Most anchors in a person's life are self-imposed. Luckily, a self-imposed anchor can also be removed by being self-aware, creating a plan, and then taking a small step toward your goal each day, as we talked about in the previous chapter.

MENTAL ANCHORS

Our self-awareness must start with understanding how we think. This impacts our attitude, which affects what we say to ourselves, which then produces results. Our minds and our belief system controls more than we realize. Think of this as our operating system for life. How many times have you worked with an old computer that continues to crash and needs to be rebooted? Once you defrag the computer and load in a new operating system, it is amazing how much better it works. The same is true in our lives. Over time, some people have developed a corrupt operating system that needs a reboot. Unfortunately, our society is worsening this problem by creating a faulty operating system in many people.

We live in a culture where many people refuse to take responsibility for their life. It is easier to blame the environment, our parents, the government, or a host of other external forces for the situation we find ourselves in. Yes, the environment and global situations can have an effect on our lives, but one of the biggest debilitating things I have witnessed are people who have a fatalistic attitude about life and feel that they are unable to control their current situation or future. In psychological terms, they have an external locus versus an internal locus of control.

A groundbreaking study by Dr. Julian B. Rotter in 1954 sought to discover if people mentally believe they can control their lives or if they believe their lives are controlled by the outside world. This study has become key in personality studies ever since. The word *locus* comes from the Latin word for place or location. In short, if you have an internal locus of control, you generally believe in self-determination—that you can control your environment by your thoughts and actions. These people tend to be less stressed, happier, and more successful. A person who has an external locus of control believes in luck and fate. They believe they are along for the ride with little ability to alter their lives with their actions or the world around them. They do not believe that they are able to change things by their actions and thus tend to have a passive stance in life, waiting for life to happen to them. Those who have an external locus of control tend to blame others and they show higher rates of stress and are more susceptible to depression. The world is full of "professional victims" who are angry at the world and blame everyone around them, yet they are never willing to look in the mirror, accept responsibility for their actions, and make changes to create a better life for themselves.

It does not take long when talking with someone to determine if they have an internal or external locus of control. To successfully operate in this new economic environment, it is important to have a positive attitude and believe that we are able to make changes and direct the course of our lives through our plans and actions. People can have many other areas of their lives in alignment and under control, but if their mental attitude and thinking is not correct, they will be unable to achieve their full potential. This is why avoiding the mental anchor is the most crucial.

Even the most positive people with an internal locus of control will go through times where hardship sets in, goals are missed, and nothing seems to work no matter what they do. During these times everyone will struggle with the feeling of helplessness and maybe even revert for a brief period to having a dire outlook on life and shifting toward an external locus of control. This is especially true for those who struggle to find a job after months of continued searching. This is when having a mentor and people to encourage you and help you stay focused is critical.

WHAT WE SAY TO OURSELVES OFTEN BECOMES REALITY.

Self-efficacy is a subset of this study and relates to our belief that we can accomplish a certain task if we put our minds to it. For example, I do not know how to ballroom dance, but if I have a high belief that with hard work I could succeed, I would be able to learn the discipline and potentially be very good at it. Because of this thought process I would be considered to have a high self-efficacy. Another example might be someone who says, "No matter how hard I try I will never be able to lose weight." This person would have a low self-efficacy, because they doubt their abilities.

Not surprisingly, what we believe usually comes true. The Bible says in Proverbs 18:21, "The tongue has the power of life and death, and those who love it will eat its fruit." There have been many self-help books written on the power of our words and thoughts in our lives. What we say to ourselves often becomes reality. I firmly believe we are able to speak life through our thoughts and words. I learned this as an athlete. If I went to the starting line in a race and thought that I couldn't win, I had already sealed my fate. I was blessed to have the opportunity to run with some of the best athletes in the world at the University of Tennessee, some of whom went on to the Olympics. The best athletes in the world prepare their minds as much as they prepare their bodies. They go through exhaustive routines to visualize for years the very moments of their competition. They preprogram everything in their minds so when the day of competition comes they have been there before, they are relaxed, and they go through the motions like they are on cruise control. As a result, their performance seems effortless. They have mentally prepared for and lived that moment thousands of times in their minds. Mental coaching and preparation is a cornerstone of every great athlete. This discipline is required in life by anyone wanting to have success.

THOSE WHO HAVE A HIGH-CONSUMPTION LIFESTYLE GENERALLY HAVE LOW INVESTMENTS AND THEREFORE HAVE FEWER OPTIONS.

If you feel that you have an external locus of control or low self-efficacy, seek out a mentor and professional for help to change your paradigm of thinking. There are many books that can help in this area. One that I have read many times and found to be helpful is *What to Say When You Talk to Your Self* by Shad Helmstetter.

Breaking down mental barriers and developing a strong internal locus of control and positive self-efficacy is important to have success in any endeavor in life. We need to take responsibility for the things we can control. We need to wake up each day with a plan and execute.

FINANCIAL ANCHORS

Financial anchors are many times self-imposed by our own actions and can be a hindrance in pursuing new opportunities. Some of the more common anchors I see affecting people include student-loan debt, car loans, mortgages, credit card debt, and lack of capital to invest in opportunities. The following graph is the most important one in this book. Those who have a high-consumption lifestyle generally have low investments and therefore have fewer options. With fewer options comes more stress. On the other hand, those who build margin in their lives but live under their means have a low-consumption lifestyle are able to invest and help others. This lifestyle produces many options and less stress.

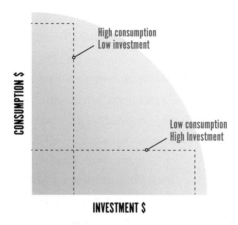

Some debt is unavoidable, such as expenses from a medical emergency that requires surgery. We can work around these, however. If you have debt, the key is to devise a plan to attack that debt burden and get debt-free as soon as possible. If you are fortunate enough to not have any debt, work hard to keep it that way.

Financially speaking, I want to encourage everyone to be debt-free with a freedom fund. It may take a long time to achieve this but this should be the goal, and with the proper plan and daily taking steps to get there it will happen sooner than you think. As I stated earlier, it is important to have a full understanding of your financial situation, and fortunately there are many tools to help us in this department. For years I have used Excel spreadsheets to create and manage my budgets and investments, but new tools have been developed that allow you to build a budget and manage your money wisely. I highly recommend Mint.com and LearnVest.com as two options that will allow you to build a program to manage your finances online with the use of mobile applications. For more special tools and calculators, use Crown's MoneyLife® Planner™ (https://planner.crown.org). Once you have all your finances grouped together in one place, you'll want to look at the debt you have. Here are a few of the common ones that present big anchors in a person's life.

STUDENT-LOAN DEBT

After the mortgage crisis of 2007, many experts said the next big bubble in the United States is student-loan debt. It is now estimated that the total outstanding student-loan debt in the United States is $1.2 trillion.[1] To put this in perspective, the total outstanding credit card debt in the United States is $854.2 billion.[2] Student debt now affects 37 million Americans and over 40 percent under the age of 35 have this form of debt.[3] Those graduating with this type of debt feel the impact for years and sometime decades. The average payments can range from $900 to $1300 a month, which means that young people are many times unable to qualify for a mortgage if they need one and they are unable to start saving for retirement. Many are graduating and, due to the economy, are not able to find full-time employment and yet are saddled with payment-due notices that start arriving in the mail within six months. I am a huge advocate of education, but I believe one should do everything possible to achieve a quality education without going into debt.

Recently a friend of mine had a daughter who was accepted into an Ivy League graduate program where she planned to study social work. The cost of this two-year program was well over $100K, and my friend asked me if this was a good investment. Upon further discussion, he told me that the starting salary in her career field would be $30,000–$40,000. I told him if *he* was willing to write a check so she could graduate debt-free, do it. However, if her plan was to fund this with student loans, only to graduate with a $30K job, have over $100K in student debt, and a long road ahead with limited earning potential in her career field, I advised against it. In my opinion, she could get a quality education for less at a state school and still have a brilliant career with much less debt. Had she been going to medical school to achieve a degree in an advanced field with a much higher salary and career potential, I would have thought differently.

The key here is to weigh the cost with the potential return on your investment. Not all educations are the same. I strongly discourage people from going into debt to get a degree from a "mail-order institution" that just churns out graduates with minimal work required. I consistently see in the real world these graduates have the letters behind their names, but the degree is almost worthless. Get the best education you can afford, and try to the best of your ability to not go into debt to fund it. Work through school and apply for as many scholarships as possible. Remember, not all degrees are equal. Although a certain degree may be easy to earn, ask yourself if it will yield the results you desire upon graduation.

AUTO LOAN DEBT

As a father of five children I understand the importance of safe and reliable transportation. Early in my marriage I drove a 1985 Volkswagen Bus with over 200,000 miles on it. Every day was filled with prayer that the vehicle would start and not break down on the way. I remember when my wife and I got our first new car and how great it felt to be able to jump in and drive around town without having to worry about it breaking down. Safe and reliable transportation can take a lot of stress out of your life. However, many people over-purchase and get the vehicle of their dreams, only to have it become a huge anchor in their life.

While I was in college, a friend told me about a business opportunity that was apparently going to make him "millions." He went out and leased a new sports car, and he was delivering pizzas in his new car when this great opportunity turned out to be a huge bust. Shortly thereafter he had to return the vehicle. We probably all have similar stories of people who made an unwise decision, only to regret it later. If we are honest with ourselves, we all have a few of our own. That is part of growing and learning in life. When possible, pay cash for a vehicle, and if you need to take out a loan, pay it off as soon as possible. Purchase a vehicle that will last a long time and will not be expensive to fix. Friends might have flashy new vehicles, but nothing is cooler than being able to say, "Mine is paid off."

I have a close friend and business partner who is a recent college graduate and doing quite well for himself. Although he could afford a very nice new vehicle, he continues to happily drive his decade-old Toyota Camry every day. Many people his age without discipline or business knowledge would have graduated and bought a nice new vehicle. He decided to use his money differently and invest it into operations that would yield a return and help him build wealth. Within the last year I watched him become an equity partner by investing in two businesses that have huge upside potential. While his friends might have a new car, he has two businesses that will start creating wealth for him. By his discipline and listening to key advisors in his life, he is already a decade or more ahead of his peers.

In the old economy, the car you drove was a status symbol that many used to portray their success. The new status symbol is being debt-free and having options. Invest wisely so that you have many options in the future.

MORTGAGE-LOAN DEBT

Other anchors like student-loan debt and auto loans are portable and will move with you, but having a mortgage many times locks a person into a locality. Mortgage debt, especially for the younger generation just starting their careers, is simply the worst debt you can have. To the recent college graduates: I highly encourage you to take a year or two out of college to start building your career and resume, and to be very certain of your future prospects within a community before making the move to purchase a home. Renting an apartment or condo gives you flexibility to be mobile. As you get older and you start a family, you will have to put down roots that will make moving become more difficult. While you are young, use mobility to your advantage.

During the collapse of 2007, many homeowners found the values of their homes diminished from one-third to one-half almost overnight. I witnessed many people who lost work in Michigan and were unable to sell their homes because of the mass exodus of people leaving the state to look for work in other parts of the country. There were many who lost their jobs, could not find work locally, were unable to make their mortgage payments, and lost their homes and all they had invested in them. Markets today can change quickly, and once you buy a home you are betting on the local economy and market to be sustainable to the foreseeable future. The two questions you have to ask yourself are: (1) If I were to lose my job, how easy would it be for me to find another one locally? (2) If I needed to sell my home so I could move to another part of the country to find work, how long would it take to sell? Remember, the answer to these questions will be different during a good economy versus a bad one. Many people were not prepared for the Great Recession that was started by the sub-prime mortgage crisis in 2007–2008.[4] This is one reason I believe it is so important to have a fully funded freedom fund with one year of available liquidity. When you commit to having that as your goal, you will work hard to keep your debt-burden and monthly burn rate as low as possible. The lower your burn rate, the easier it is to have a fully funded freedom fund. Housing expenses tend to be the most expensive line item in most people's monthly budgets, so this is an important item to get right. As a rule of thumb, your housing should be less than 25 percent of your total monthly burn rate.

CREDIT CARD DEBT

Credit card debt is the most insidious form of debt and the most damaging if not controlled with strict discipline. The good news is that, with a plan, you can quickly take steps to get rid of this. I think this is the most important debt to address if you have multiple forms of debt. For example, if you have a student loan, a car loan, and credit card debt, I would suggest you formulate a plan to pay your monthly minimums on your student loans and car loans, and put every extra penny you have toward your credit card debt. This is assuming that your credit card debt has the highest interest rate of the three, and most often that is the case.

There are many ways to start paying down credit card debt. Larry Burkett, the founder of Crown, started encouraging people to understand what it meant to be a proper steward of what God has blessed us with. He encouraged people to live debt-free and developed a program to help people achieve this goal. Crown has been teaching people for over 38 years how to organize their debt and pay it off with the *snowball method*. There are many national personalities who have applied this method and have helped millions of people. The basic idea is to collect all your credit card debt, pay the minimum payment on all your cards, and put any extra money down on the card with the lowest balance until you pay it off. This helps build momentum. Then you move on to the credit card with the next lowest amount, and pay that one off. You continue with this system until you have no more credit card debt. The psychology of this is that people are motivated by seeing improvement and progress. As we make a plan and start executing on it each day, it is encouraging to see how we are reducing our spending and making progress to get debt-free. Here is an example of a debt snowball:

		ENTRY COLUMNS			CALCULATED COLUMNS	
#	CREDITOR	PRINCIPLE BALANCE	INTEREST RATE (%)	PAYMENT AMOUNT ($)	INTEREST COST	# OF PMTS LEFT
1	Gap	190	19	190		1
2	Amazon	220	23	20		13
3	Visa	1,200	14	30		55
4	Car Loan	3,600	21	80		90
5	Student Loan	11,000	5	150		88

Adapted from Crown (www.crown.org/FindHelp/Personal/Calculators DebtSnowball.aspx)

Now some experts have come forward and said this system works, but that a potentially better way to pay off your credit card debts would be to organize the payments based on the highest interest rate, not the lowest balance. By paying off the highest interest rate first and then moving down the line, you would save money. This was the way my wife and I paid off our credit card debt in the late 1990s, before I knew of the snowball method. At the time this seemed most logical—pay off my highest interest rates first and then move down the line. Both methods work, but the key is to have a plan and to stay consistent and disciplined. The psychology of the debt snowball system is proven: people do get motivated when they see a card paid off, and this builds excitement and more discipline to stay focused and not give up. Whichever way you choose, the critical aspect is that you pick a method and stay the course.

The next question many people ask is, Should I even have a credit card? Many programs will say that every credit card should be cut up and that you should pay cash for everything. I agree with not carrying credit card debt. I also think that having or not having a credit card is a personal choice, but I think there are many reasons why having a credit card and using it wisely is okay. Because I travel overseas and have a personal business, I use my credit card every day, but I also make it a habit to pay it off each month. By doing this I have special perks that American Express offers me,

INSTEAD OF CUTTING UP A CREDIT CARD AND THINKING THE PROBLEM IS SOLVED, THE KEY IS TO GO DEEPER AND TRULY ADDRESS THE ROOT OF THE PROBLEM.

like free airline tickets, insurance on my purchases, etc. These are things I would not have if using a debit card or cash. It is all about discipline and self-control. That is the root issue. If you have discipline you can use a credit card and be perfectly okay. If you don't have discipline and self-control, not using credit cards might help you in some respects. But your lack of discipline and self-control will manifest itself in other areas. Instead of cutting up a credit card and thinking the problem is solved, the key is to go deeper and truly address the root of the problem.

For those who have credit card debt and feel like they need help putting a plan together, I highly recommend Christian Credit Counselors. This is a non-profit organization that has been helping people for over 20 years. They have multiple programs that will help people analyze their situation, including a "Turbo-Charged Debt Snowball," which helps people pay off their credit card debt faster than most other programs. To learn more go to www. ChristianCreditCounselors.org. Use the code "The Leap" to get a free debt-assessment.

PHYSICAL ANCHORS

If you are blessed with good health, do not take this for granted. In fact, no matter the stage of life you are currently in, one of the first action plans you should put in place today is steps to improve and protect your health! As health care costs continue to rise, a larger percentage of household income is going toward health care. For example, a recent report shows that Medicare participants on average spend 14 percent of their income on health care-related costs, and this is expected to rise significantly in the years to come. The same survey showed that non-Medicare participants spent on average 9 percent of their income on health care.[5]

As everyone plans for retirement, a key thing to remember is that as we age, our health is going to be a big driver in the quality of life. Poor health will also become one of our biggest expenses later in life, which will drastically affect retirement savings. Later in this book we will focus on developing multiple income streams and strategies to prepare for retirement. Avoiding physical anchors early and late in life is a key to success. Health anchors can slowly develop over time without you realizing it. As life becomes busier with multiple obligations, high-stress jobs, and a fast-paced lifestyle that never seems to slow down, it is easy to jettison a healthy lifestyle. There is never a good excuse for this. It is a dangerous precedent to set, and once an unhealthy lifestyle becomes the norm, it is hard to break.

Some of the best advice I received early in my career was from a mentor who said, "Bob, in everything you do, pay yourself first." He gave the example of investing for retirement and my physical health. He said, "Get up in the morning and get your exercise in for the day. Then go to work and give it 100 percent. If you wait until the end of the day to exercise, many times you will come home having given 100 percent at work and will be too tired to work out. When that happens, you cheat yourself. Likewise, when you get paid, automatically have a draft that goes into an investment account that you don't touch, then pay all your bills. If you craft your budget around your current needs and desires and only invest what is left over, you will never invest."

Don't allow your future to be taken care of last after every other obligation in your life. Ensure you pay yourself first by taking care of yourself, and protecting your health. Our daily routines add up over the years and will dictate our quality of life down the road. There is no special pill that can undo a lifetime of bad habits. If we do not take care of ourselves in our youth and through every stage of life, we will end up paying the price late in life with low quality of life and extremely high health care costs that will dramatically impact our retirement.

However, physical anchors won't just impact us late in life, they can impact us today. In the new economy people are being asked to do more with less. Employees are working longer hours and many are forced to wear multiple hats as they perform the jobs of two or three positions, as companies are unable or unwilling to fully staff. The only way to successfully navigate that type of environment is to be healthy. A physically fit and active person with a healthy diet will generally have more energy and be more alert than his sedentary coworker who is living an unhealthy lifestyle. Over time, the healthy worker will out-perform the others, which will lead to more opportunities and pay raises. A healthy and active person puts himself in a virtuous cycle, whereas the unhealthy coworker puts himself in a doom loop. Again, this is another example where our personal decisions and actions affect our lives, and those with an internal locus of control see that their actions can set a course for success.

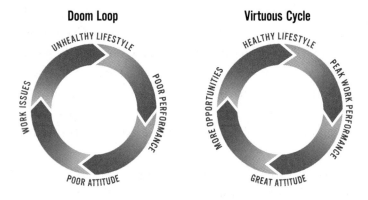

SPIRITUAL ANCHORS

One of the most damaging anchors we can carry through life is one of spiritual misalignment. I don't think there is anything more disabling than being spiritually misaligned. As a follower of Christ I feel profound fulfillment in my life when living out my values at work and at home. The times in life when I have experienced depression were the times when I was not living out my values and I was out of balance. We all will go through rough times in our life when we will be tested, and it will require every ounce of strength and faith we have to get through a day. It is during those times when my faith has grown the most and God has shown His mercy and love to me, undeserving as I am. In my life, I can say that I have experienced answered prayer, seen miraculous things happen, felt the presence of God, and come to a place where I have a personal relationship with Christ that is meaningful to me in every way.

IT IS IMPORTANT TO ENJOY THE PEOPLE YOU WORK WITH AND HAVE A CULTURE THAT IS POSITIVE AND IN ALIGNMENT WITH WHO YOU ARE AND WHAT YOU VALUE.

Since about 50 percent of your waking hours each day will be in a work environment, it is important to enjoy the people you work with and have a culture that is positive and in alignment with who you are and what you value. In the past, this was not at the top of a job seeker's needs, but today the millennial generation is changing that paradigm and is seeking out work environments that provide a lifestyle-based and values-based culture that inspires them. This is translating to older generations nearing retirement asking the same questions. People are leaving toxic corporate cultures because of poor leadership and destructive people. If you are in that situation, don't be afraid to take the leap. You will find better employment elsewhere and be happier in a less stressful environment where your values are in alignment.

As we navigate these difficult situations, there is no doubt that there are circumstances that we cannot control. We can't control the economy or acts of God, but we can control our response. We can control many aspects of our lives and our attitudes in dealing with these obstacles. Our reactions and how we prepare for these events and take action will have great impact on how successful we will be.

Over the past year, I have worked with young and old alike who are navigating this economy and have been frustrated at some of the self-imposed anchors that hinder them from making great leaps.

It is painful to watch these self-created anchors hold them hostage in a situation of pain when they could take the leap to a better environment. Some of the common phrases I have heard that hold people back are:

- I don't want to leave this city.
- I need to live near my family.
- I can't sell my house.
- I need to make a certain amount of money, so I can't take that new position because it would be a step backward, even though in the long run it would be a greater opportunity for me.
- This sounds like a great opportunity, but I was looking for something else, and this sounds like a difficult assignment.
- I'm scared to try that.

The list goes on. The above list are reasons ("anchors") why an individual is unable to make the leap to a new career or new job when the possibility is right in front of them. These typically come from someone who has not developed a game plan and does not have a real understanding of the economy and a deep self-awareness and what they want out of life. Those self-aware individuals who have developed a plan are able to thoughtfully analyze a situation and make timely decisions in the best interest of their family and career without stress because they are operating from alignment and a predetermined objective.

DON'T BUILD YOURSELF A PRISON

The discussion I had with my "successful" friend many years ago might resonate with some mid-career professionals who worked in their 20s and 30s to achieve their dreams, only to arrive at a spot in life where they feel trapped on a treadmill they can't jump off of. The obligations mount each day as pressures of life continue to build, and maybe you wonder if things would be different had you made different decisions years earlier. Looking in the rearview mirror is no way to live life. You can't change the past but you can change your future by the decisions you make today and the action that you take tomorrow.

My friend had created anchors in his life that became a prison. He was on a career path he could not change because of his lifestyle. He was unwilling to change his lifestyle and so his high monthly burn rate to support multiple homes, boats, and the overhead to keep it all going was at the forefront of his mind daily. It consumed his every waking minute. He was unable to enjoy life. He had crafted a public perception of success, and he could not walk away from this life. He had created his own prison that he could not escape although he was talented in many other areas and could have been successful at many things. To this day, with a smile on his face and cheerful greeting to those around him, he labors down that path but is quietly unhappy and unfulfilled every minute of the day.

THE WORST ANCHOR IS THAT OF REGRET.

The pursuit of material success many times creates a prison that we cannot escape. Some of the most unhappy people I have encountered are the ones who had the goal of chasing success in terms of amassing material wealth, career achievements, and personal fame. Although there is nothing wrong with those things per se, they alone are hollow and will not provide a real sense of achievement and long-lasting happiness. I have found the happiest people are the ones who live a balanced life with a desire to make a difference in the world and help people around them. In this case, they have an external view of the world. They see first how they can help others and support their community. The outward-looking view in this realm provides them with inner peace and a sense of achievement that cannot be had by any other means.

The worst anchor is that of regret. Some of my most heartbreaking moments have been watching someone in the final stages of their life as they look back with regret, wishing they could do it all over again and knowing they made terrible mistakes they can never undo. As you develop your plan in life and work to avoid anchors both in youth and in old age, begin with the end in mind and think about where you want to be when it is all said and done. If you achieve your goals and dreams, will it have made a difference? Will your life have mattered? Did you make the world a better place? Ask any follower of Christ around the globe what they one day hope to hear when they die and go to heaven and almost everyone will answer with, "Well done, good and faithful servant!" Live your life in such a way that one day you will hear these words!

HOW TO STAY FLEXIBLE

With that said, here is my parting advice on avoiding anchors in your life. I have seen these five items to be big anchors that hinder people from seizing great opportunities in front of them.

1) DEBT | Work hard to stay out of debt. The more debt you have, the less flexible you are and the fewer options you have available to you.

2) GEOGRAPHY | Don't lock yourself into a location early in your career. Be willing to move often to take new jobs and advance within your company or industry.

3) MORTGAGES | When you do decide to buy a home, be careful. It is possible, when the time is right, to purchase a home and have it be an investment and not an anchor in your life. Work with your mentor and get multiple points of counsel to make a good decision.

4) LACK OF LONG-TERM PLAN | Craft a long-term plan and put it on paper. Have goals along the way that you actively work toward. If you are married, have an understanding with your spouse on what level of flexibility and risk-taking you both feel is okay for your family. Both partners need to be on the same page. Have a plan and be working on it together.

5) LACK OF LIQUIDITY | Maintain a cash reserve. In business they say, "Cash is king." In your life, cash equals flexibility. Having a freedom fund that is liquid with at least one year of your current burn rate saved up allows you to take some risks and also live without the stress of trying to make it to your next paycheck.

Start with self-awareness of your skills, passions, and goals. Then, work to avoid anchors. This will help you as you start your career as well as help you transition and progress throughout your career. There is nothing I enjoy more than seeing someone operate within their sweet spot, be passionate about what they do, and help others do the same.

As you take the leap at the beginning of your career or later in life, there are many that you can emulate as a role model. In the old economy, wealth and success were many times measured by material possessions like homes, vehicles, boats, what you wear, and all the traditional trappings of success that lead people to constantly grasp for more. In the new economy, those with a well-balanced understanding of life realize that true wealth is measured by what we give, not what we receive. True success is about freedom and having options that come from a debt-free lifestyle, enabling us to live unencumbered and with the ability to be focused on making a difference in the world.

Leaping by Example

AVOIDING ANCHORS: Jeremie Kubicek, *GiANT, cofounder and CEO*

....

It was at a Young Presidents' Organization forum that Jeremie Kubicek, cofounder and CEO of GiANT, announced to a small group, "I've decided to step down as CEO of GiANT. I'm hiring someone else to run the company. My family and I are selling everything we own, and we are moving to London to start a new business venture." The news was shocking; GiANT had seen incredible success under Jeremie. The GiANT Leadercast sold out to over 10,000 people in Atlanta and was simulcast to hundreds of locations around the world to over 150,000 people. Catalyst, the largest leadership event for young, faith-based leaders in North America, pulled in similar numbers. But for Jeremie, it was time for something new. And his leap began as he ditched every anchor in his life to follow his dream.

"I learned that you really don't need much. Some clothing, a toothbrush, a Bible, and your family. It has changed our entire world. We basically got out of the rat race so we could focus on giving ourselves away for others."

Jeremie's thoughts on anchors: "Self-preservation is the overprotection of what you are afraid of losing. I find that most young couples begin to create inhibitors in their lives around what they are afraid of losing or what they are trying to prove to others. These inhibitors make people immobile. It is human nature to acquire things that are useful in everyday life. And yet we realize things become less important over time, whereas relationships become more important. After moving to England, we began to take on the European view of meals, which basically means long, lingering meals. Meals to Europeans are the event. They are not trying to cram dinner, movie, and coffee into one evening—they are investing in relationships. That is our biggest takeaway. Humans need fewer things, but more relationships that are deeper."

Here are Jeremie's five keys to success:

1. Don't slum to the world's standards of acquiring. They don't bring real life.
2. Focus on deepening relationships; they last far past things.
3. Invest and save. Just do it. It works and you will be glad you did later.
4. Understand your personality type early and lead yourself based on who you really are.
5. If you are looking for a job, find the person you want to work for, not the title of the job. People will take you places that jobs never will.

STICKING THE LANDING

- Have a clear understanding of your current financial situation. Register with Mint.com or Learnvest.com to have an online tool to track all your finances.

- If you have debt, take steps to reduce it as quickly as possible. Put a plan in place to be debt-free. If you have credit card debt that you're struggling to pay off, contact Christian Credit Counselors.

- Start building your freedom fund. Download your free Excel spreadsheet from www.RobertDickie.com to track your monthly burn rate and see how quickly you can build your freedom fund.

CHAPTER 4

DEVELOP YOUR MUSCLES

"Action is the foundational key to all success." —PABLO PICASSO

Mike Tyson is famous for saying that everyone has a plan until they get punched in the face. Tyson and his coach probably knew all the moves his opponents would try in order to defeat him, but one after one, early in his career, he dispatched them with ease. Likewise, German Field Marshall Helmuth Karl Bernhard Graf Von Moltke, considered one of the greatest military strategists in the 19th century, is famous for saying, "No plan survives first contact with the enemy!" If having a plan is so critical to success, why do the greatest boxer and military strategist of their respective generations allude to plans being ineffective? The answer lies in human nature.

As we spoke about this in the last chapter, it is critical for us to develop a success plan for multiple areas of our life. For us to be successful, however, we need to build the muscle and discipline to stay focused on our goal. Whether you are in the boxing ring or in a military battle, all plans need to be flexible and adapt to an ever-changing, fluid environment. Both Mike Tyson and Field Marshall

Moltke understand that many people have a plan, but when adversity hits, those plans usually get tossed. There is a big difference between ditching a plan because of lack of discipline, and pivoting and making adjustments to a plan to have success. However, before we can worry about making alterations to a plan, we first have to understand why so many people fail to stay focused on the plan to begin with.

A PROGRAM FOR PROGRESS

Attend any self-help seminar and an analogy commonly shared is the phenomenon of the New Year's resolution crowd who so eagerly pile into their local gyms with excitement and enthusiasm to achieve their goals of losing weight and getting in shape. This has become somewhat of a joke for the disciplined patrons who experience this January rush each year. The "regulars" who take their physical fitness seriously and train year-round joke that they may get frustrated with the crowded space at the gym but only have to wait 30 days to see people quickly lose sight of the goal and start dropping off. How do we ensure that the goals we are setting as we take the leap don't end up on a list of many unaccomplished goals in life? We need to have intense focus and daily dedication to our goals. Actually, these are key characteristics of anyone who has achieved success in any area of life. Consider Olympic athletes who will train for years for a single event that might only take minutes or a few seconds to complete. They are willing to invest years of dedication and preparation for one moment in time. You may not be training for the Olympics, but your goals and dreams are just as important. If you follow the same discipline and intense focus of an Olympic athlete you will be well on your way to a great reward.

> **HOW DO WE ENSURE THAT THE GOALS WE ARE SETTING AS WE TAKE THE LEAP DON'T END UP ON A LIST OF MANY UNACCOMPLISHED GOALS IN LIFE?**

When I was in the Air Force, I was transferred to Hickam Air Force Base–Hawaii shortly after 9/11. I had been a runner in college at the University of Tennessee but had since taken some time off from competitive running and wasn't in great shape anymore. Soon after arriving in Honolulu, my friend Gary wanted me to start running with his group, which was training for a marathon. He hooked me up with his coach, Farley, who developed a training program that would slowly build me up to be able to handle the training mileage. The first few practices were an embarrassment. Athletes from around the island came together early Sunday morning to do their weekly long run. The standard distance was 18 miles on the Honolulu Marathon course, which they covered with ease while chatting with each other. I barely mustered six miles, struggling through the heat and months of inactivity that left me in terrible shape. Gary and Farley continued to encourage me and told me to stay with the plan. They said, "Don't worry, Bob. Trust us, in a few months you will be running those 18-milers with us. You can do it." Had I tried to do this on the very first day it would have ended badly. However, over a yearlong process of building my muscles I was slowly able to run longer and faster than I ever had before. In sports science it is called the *super compensation curve*.

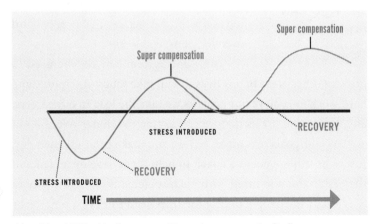

Adapted from MC Nutrition (www.mc-nutrition.net/supercompensation.html)

The human body is an adaptable organism that acclimates to its environment. Therefore, the theory states that you start with a certain level of fitness. You undergo a training session that stresses the muscles, after which you recover and your body "compensates" for the stress. After your rest period, your body has a higher state of fitness. The four stages are:

- Initial fitness
- Training (induced stress)
- Recovery (rest)
- Super compensation (growth)

As an athlete continually goes through this cycle over long periods of time, they are able to build great fitness. Any athletic discipline uses a similar type of program to gain fitness. Body builders build mass, swimmers improve their times, and distance runners can run farther and faster, all using a system of training hard, incorporating rest days, and completing the cycle month after month, sometimes for years, to become the best in the world. Gary and Farley used this system with me and over two years took me from never having run a marathon before to me running the Boston Marathon and finishing as the third American and twenty-third overall. The system works!

PEOPLE TAKING THE LEAP NEED TO HAVE A MENTOR OR "LIFE COACH" WHO CAN HELP THEM ALONG THE WAY.

The same system can also be used to grow in other areas of our lives. It will take focus, discipline, and hard work to achieve our goals as we take the leap in our careers, and these are muscles that we can exercise each day. We will not achieve our goals overnight, but we can make progress each day. Just as an athlete needs a coach to help them develop a plan and then keep them focused with encouragement along the way as they progress, people taking the leap need to have a mentor or "life coach" who can help them along the way. The key is to have someone who knows your plans and will help hold you accountable along the way with encouragement and advice.

MEET THE GOALS

Just as practice makes perfect and an athlete over time gains fitness by continuing to stress their system, those looking to achieve goals in their life need to stress their system daily as they build discipline and momentum toward their goals. With every passing day they will get stronger, more capable, and continually get closer to their goals. Many times making the plan is the easy part but it is in the execution that we fail. This is especially true when our plan will require years of hard work. The effort of putting our plan down on paper is pretty easy. It is an important step, but I have seen many athletes and business leaders create plans without the discipline to execute them daily. It is easy to start but after a while life will always get in the way and if we are not focused we will start to lose sight of the goal. How committed are you to your goal? This is why daily action toward the goal is critical. When these daily actions become life habits, we are well on our way, but how do we make these habits in our life? Most people want to be fit and live a healthy life, but the habit of rising early and exercising in the morning before you start the day is a hard habit for many to form. How do you start?

Columbia graduate and cosmetic surgeon Dr. Maxwell Maltz wrote *Psycho-Cybernetics* in 1960 and mentioned his observation of the 21-day cycle for change.

It usually requires a minimum of about 21 days to effect any perceptible change in a mental image. Following plastic surgery it takes about 21 days for the average patient to get used to his new face. When an arm or leg is amputated, the "phantom limb" persists for about 21 days. People must live in a new house for about three weeks before it begins to "feel like home." These, and many other commonly observed phenomena, tend to show that it requires a minimum of about 21 days for an old mental image to dissolve and a new one to be established.

Thus the theory that it would take about 21 days to form a new habit was born. Dr. Maltz is seen as the forerunner of the modern-day self-help movement, although no real studies have confirmed that it takes 21 days to form habits. It goes without saying that if you can do anything for 21 days straight you are on your way to forming a habit. Others have taken a different approach to trying to understand habit formation and how to coach people to break through the phase where most people quit to reach the other side where success resides.

Many coaches and self-help gurus have come up with their multi-step processes to help people understand how a habit is formed and to fight through the challenging middle where people tend to lose focus and motivation. It is during these stages where the vast majority fall out and never accomplish their goals. Dr. Tom Bartow calls the middle the "fight-through stage"[1] and tells people to first recognize that everyone goes through this. From the most accomplished athlete to the most successful businessperson, everyone goes through this challenging stage where discouragement sets in and people want to slack off or take a break. Maybe the goal seems too hard or even impossible to achieve.

Dr. Bartow has his clients ask the next question. "How will I feel if I accomplish this? How will I feel if I don't?" The next step in this phase is to imagine what your future will look like having accomplished or not accomplished your goal. This visualization helps a goal become reality in your mind. As I stated in the previous chapter, our self-talk and thoughts have the power to become reality in our life. If we focus on the negative we will create that environment. If we focus on the positive and believe it can happen and take daily steps to achieve our goal we can do that as well. In life, our words and actions can become a self-fulfilling prophecy. Dr. Jason Selk is a personal coach who has worked with many top athletes and executives around the world. He teaches that mental toughness during these stages is a great predictor of success in any endeavor in life. He says that mental toughness is defined as "your ability to stay focused on the solution and execute those solutions when it is toughest."[2]

My father always told me that everyone wants to win on race day but the race is really won in the off-season. In Michigan, training during the brutal winters is not fun but those who put in the hard work on those dark and cold winter evenings are the ones

ARE YOUR GOALS BIG ENOUGH AND IMPORTANT ENOUGH TO YOU TO TRAIN THROUGH THE DARK, COLD WINTER NIGHTS WHEN NO ONE IS AROUND CHEERING FOR YOU?

who win conference championships on sunny spring afternoons. Are your goals big enough and important enough to you to train through the dark, cold winter nights when no one is around cheering for you? If they are, you will achieve the victory you desire. Remember, everyone is motivated on game day, but the champions are the ones who put in the work when others had many good excuses not to.

Creating a plan is the first step. Taking action on that plan is the second step. To be successful we need to have continued focus and take action daily even when we get tired and discouraged and when the results seem so far off—maybe even years away. This is when we need to have our coaches and mentors around us to encourage us and remind us of our goal and how it will feel when we accomplish it. They are the ones who can help us hit our long-term goal by ensuring our small daily goals are helping us take steps in the right direction. Our daily goals must be able to be measured at the end of the day. If you can't measure it, you can't track it. Here is an example of some small daily goals that might help someone reach bigger, longer-term goals in their life. Notice how each one can be measured by an action at the end of a day.

DAILY GOALS

HEALTH | Wake each morning at 5 a.m. to exercise. Do 30 minutes of cardio five days a week with 10 minutes of stretching and one set of core routine to follow. Be in bed by 9 p.m. each night to get eight hours of sleep. (Reason: 5k race in three months. Live a healthy life to reduce health care costs later in life.)

FINANCES | No eating out. No discretionary spending. Follow your budget, with no other items purchased. Focus all income on paying down credit card debt and fully funding your freedom fund! (Reason: Get out of debt, gain peace of mind, and have more options available to me at all times.)

EDUCATION | Finish three courses on Khan Academy and Codecademy and take notes. Read two chapters in my continuing education book. (Reason: Learn key skill sets to help me advance in my job for future promotions and pay increases.)

CAREER | Send at least two emails to contacts in my network to stay in touch. Review my LinkedIn account to see if anyone is asking for help. Respond with a tip or put them in touch with someone who can help them. (Reason: Develop my network. Help others. Make myself known to other companies who might want to recruit me to join their team.)

YOU NEED A VERY BIG *WHY* THAT MOTIVATES YOU AT THE CORE OF YOUR BEING.

These are just some examples but you get the picture. The goals must be something that can be done that day. They must be things that you can take action on, and at the end of the day you have the satisfaction of having checked them off the list. You also need to know exactly how each activity impacts your ability to achieve your long-term goal. Why are you doing this? You need a very big *why* that motivates you at the core of your being. When this becomes very emotional to you and you can mentally visualize achieving your goal, you will be unstoppable.

It is very encouraging to look back at the end of the week and see your progress. I encourage people to track this daily, weekly, and monthly. If you miss your goal, make adjustments in your life and start over. Here is a little secret: you won't hit your goals every week. No one does, even the most successful Olympic athletes and executives. The key is to have a goal and be taking action each day on it, tracking the results and making micro adjustments along the way.

Imagine looking back at the end of a week to see all the miles you have run, the money you saved by not eating out, the debt that you were able to pay down, the advancement in your education, and the 14 people who you made contact with throughout the week and potentially helped. You have to be able to measure and track it. If you can't, your goal is not granular enough. This is not easy, and it will take time and work. However, most goals worth accomplishing are not easy and will require daily action to achieve them. Start today by building your muscle and developing the discipline to make little goals and achieve them. Over time you will gain momentum and you will be amazed at how quickly you are able to accomplish the bigger goals in your life.

After you make your plan, start avoiding anchors in life, and exercise the daily development of creating habits that will help you reach your goals, it is time to start developing your network of relationships around the world.

Leaping by Example

BUILDING YOUR MUSCLE: Kevin Thompson, *Thompson Burton PLLC cofounder and president*

Kevin Thompson decided to take the leap during the Great Recession to start his own law firm in Nashville. With a pregnant wife and a child in tow, he moved from Michigan and started his journey. Starting his practice from his new home in Nashville, his business grew and he partnered with Walt Burton to form Thompson Burton PLLC with the goal to "Redefine the Art of Law." With 11 full-time attorneys and their supporting staff, they are a rising darling in the legal profession, receiving accolades from clients. They even have Vanderbilt law professors seeking them out to understand how they are changing from the old paradigm long practiced by traditional law firms.

Kevin had developed the muscle over the years to undertake this type of leap when others would have been fearful to start. Facing adversity was not something Kevin shied away from; it actually inspired him to action. A former All-American decathlete from the University of Tennessee, Kevin understands the concept of developing muscle athletically to aid in performance and how it carries over to the business world as well. "Just like in sports where athletes invest time in developing muscle, professionals need to invest time in building their 'professional muscle' to ensure they're equipped to handle the challenges. It takes daily commitment to accrue the gains necessary over time before a professional is really ready to take the leap." As someone who built the required muscle to make the leap, Kevin offered four qualities that helped him and that he looks for in others who he is inviting to join him and his team.

1. Leadership: Identify a problem that troubles you and start solving it. Do something. Anything! When I see a candidate who has done nothing except school their whole life I think, "What's your excuse? There are plenty of problems in the world that need solving, and this is a great way to grow your leadership while making a difference."

2. Points of difference: Get some accolades outside of academia. In my opinion, college is a controlled environment. The marketplace is chaotic. I want to see some results, good or bad, from a candidate in the marketplace. I personally need people that can learn fast, adapt fast, and strive for progress over perfection.

3. Patience: Success is the result of good habits compounding over time. If I know they have good habits, I know the results will soon follow.

4. Make a plan: Be intentional with your decisions. If you're not happy, dig a trench to the exit. Try to find something you enjoy. Without passion the quality of your work will be mediocre and the quality of your life will be dismal. When making your plan remember that debt eliminates options, and options are necessary when building a life.

STICKING THE LANDING

- Put your goals in multiple spots where you will see them each day. This might be on the mirror in your bathroom, on the dashboard of your vehicle, on your phone, or as the screen saver on your computer. Be reminded of them daily and take small steps toward achieving them.

- Have your advisor hold you accountable for your progress. Schedule a monthly meeting where you will report on how you are doing.

- Stay positive. Understand that you might work for months and even years toward your goal. You won't get there overnight but if you stay focused and take action daily, before long you will look back and be surprised at how much progress you have made.

CHAPTER 5

GROW
YOUR
INCOME

*"Formal education will make you a living; self education
will make you a fortune."* —JIM ROHN

As the dust settled from the crash of 2008, global citizens were
still dazed after witnessing the unthinkable, the collapse of insti-
tutions where trust and security had been placed for generations.
This ushered in a new reality that people could hardly understand.
The paper statements and online reports showing 401(k) balances,
portfolio assets, net worth assessments, and real-estate values had
all been revalued almost overnight. The fortunate few talked about
losses of 25 percent. Many spoke of retirement plans being cut in
half while others spoke of total loss, which either meant the loss of a
job or an entire lifetime of savings or both.

Many of us watched from afar, years earlier, as companies like
Enron, WorldCom, and Global Crossing failed. We saw images of
stunned and crying employees walking into the streets carrying
boxes of mementos from their offices, in total disbelief that their
company, job, and sometimes life savings tied up in company

stock were gone overnight. As we watched the evening news, we convinced ourselves we were immune to these catastrophes. We rationalized these rare events were due to the mismanagement of greedy corporate officials and misdeeds of a few, and that *our* companies would never suffer this fate. We numbed ourselves with the fact that government intervention and regulation would protect *us* from this kind of disaster. Then one morning we woke up and Bear Stearns, Washington Mutual, and Lehman Brothers were gone with Bank of America, Goldman Sachs, and others fighting for their lives. Once-iconic companies of the American economy like GM were on life support. What happened? The world changed overnight and our collective futures with it.

BECOMING A FREE AGENT AND WORKING IN THE "ECONO-ME" IS A GROWING OPTION FOR PEOPLE.

The world has been changing all around us for many years, but it has been in small increments, and we have not seen the impacts. However, the economic downturn in 2008 was the watershed event that, like a receding tide, exposed all the items once covered by water, and the landscape became clearer for the onlooker. Lifelong employment with companies and the perceived security those jobs provided became a relic of the past. Technology has been advancing at a rapid rate, changing the way businesses operate. The traditional corporate office is going the way of Blockbuster. Radical changes are occurring that impact the way people work and live. There have been negative effects for sure, but it has also provided a way for the adventurous and hardworking to take advantage of these advancements and participate in the growing free-agent economy, or as I call it: the Economy of Me, or EconoME.

Roughly 16 percent of the United States population (25 million people) now participate in the EconoME as some type of free agent. Over 14 million are considered self-employed, 8.3 million are independent contractors, and 2.3 million work for temporary agencies. Last year 74 million Americans received an IRS Form 1099, the typical pay method for a free agent. Becoming a free agent and working in the EconoME is a growing option for people. *New York Times* bestselling author of *A Whole New Mind* and *Free Agent Nation*, Daniel Pink, says, "Freedom is the pathway to security, not a detour from it!"[1] So how can you take the leap and start building a side business that is producing income that could one day be your full-time endeavor?

Many people do not even want to try because it seems too risky. We have been convinced that we can live in a world without risk. We are offered insurance for everything and we are educated about safe careers, guaranteed retirements, and risk-free lives, but it is all a false sense of security at best and sometimes an outright lie as this security is just a myth.

The Bible says this is a temporal world and that nothing accumulated here will last. With these recent events, many people are seeing how fleeting success and material things really are.

In this chapter, we are discussing how to have success in your career. I have found that some Christian leaders are afraid to even mention the word success and have it be a part of their vocabulary, fearing it treads closely to a worldview of materialism. I differ in my thinking. I think it is important to be successful in all we do. I believe we are called by God to give our best in all endeavors in life and strive for success. I am not advocating chasing a secular view of success by building up material possessions and achieving success for self-gratification. I believe our purpose is much greater . . . to make a difference in the world and in the lives of those around us. As a student and follower of Christ, I firmly believe the greatest success we can have is a true relationship with Him and understanding that our time on this earth is but a blink of an eye. My goal is to help people navigate this new economy, make a difference in the

> **HAVING MULTIPLE SOURCES OF INCOME IS THE BEST INSURANCE YOU CAN HAVE.**

world, be able to provide for their families, and be able to support others in times of need. To do this we need to be prepared. One of the most important things to do as we look to build a full-time life in this new part-time world is to diversify our income streams just as we would diversify our investments and retirement plans. This is a critical step in our plan to build a successful life in this new world. Having multiple sources of income is the best insurance you can have. The way to achieve this goal is to dust off your entrepreneurial skills and start building a side business today. But before you work on building other revenue streams for your family, if you still are working full-time, make sure you are maximizing your earning potential with your current company by negotiating your pay.

PAY RATES AND COMPENSATION AGREEMENTS

Recent studies are confirming what many working Americans felt from 2000 to 2012: wages remained flat even though prices on everything from gasoline to milk continued to rise. The average American in this environment is falling behind each year regarding their purchasing power. Two staff members from the Economic Policy Institute, Lawrence Mishel and economist Heidi Shierholz, analyzed this in great detail in their paper, "A Decade of Flat Wages." A key finding in this report highlights that while productivity was up 7.7 percent from 2007 to 2012, the bottom 70 percent of the workforce saw wage decreases during the recession.[2] This startling fact has many economists calling 2000 to 2010 the "Lost Decade" for the American working class. There are many who have endured cutbacks, hiring freezes, downsizing, years without pay raises, and cost of living adjustments. For those people who are thinking about adding extra revenue streams for their family, the first place to start is a conversation with their current supervisor about their compensation. If, for some time now, you have been doing a great job for your employer, creating value every day for your workplace, and have been a key performer on your team yet have not had a pay raise or cost of living adjustment, it is time to sit down with your boss and have a frank discussion.

The poet Robert Frost wrote in "Mending Wall," "Good fences make good neighbors."[3] In business, I have come to find that good compensation agreements make for good employment—and not just for top executives. They act as a barrier to misunderstanding and a boundary against *mission creep*. In an employee setting, mission creep is when your roles and responsibilities over time continue to grow. The same level of excellence is placed on you but potentially with fewer resources. To keep up, you just work longer hours and endure more stress, and everyone quietly accepts it as the status quo as a condition of the employee. Although there are times and even long periods where this may be necessary for an organization to overcome a temporary challenge, if you feel that you have sustained mission creep in your job that has become the status quo, you need to schedule a meeting with your supervisor and discuss a remedy. Many people are okay with added workload and responsibilities but they also want to be fairly compensated for it.

When starting new employment arrangements, in fact, all employees need compensation and employment agreements, as everyone benefits from clear goals and identified rewards for meeting metrics that bring value to the company.

WISE PROFESSIONALS RELY ON CONTRACTS AND WILL RESPECT YOU FOR NEGOTIATING YOURS.

If a potential employer acts offended that you request an employment or compensation agreement, proceed with caution. Most supervisors will respect an employee who requests to discuss their compensation agreement and how to add metrics for growth that is a win both for the company and for the employee. Also, it may be good for your employer to know you have other employment options. Having options gives you the freedom to not only demand to be fairly compensated for your work but also to leave a poor work environment if needed.

Wise professionals rely on contracts and will respect you for negotiating yours. Often the person who does not want to be encumbered with a document is planning to change the arrangement in their favor later. A signed contract protects all parties, and in particular protects an employee from unexpected accountabilities. While it is not common for everyone to have an employment contract, you should have in writing the deal points you have agreed on.

Case in point: me. One of my first big mistakes in business was relying on promises made in a handshake deal. Conversations can be heard and remembered differently, especially by those who do not have integrity and look to take advantage of a situation. Learn from my mistakes and remember the seven key areas to negotiate on your compensation agreement.

1) COMPENSATION | This includes base salary, commissions potential, and bonus structure. Know how and when each will be paid, and have this clearly annotated. Start your negotiations with base salary and move into the other areas in sequential order. If base pay is set, immediately consider other incentives.

2) WORKING ARRANGEMENTS | If your employer says they are unable to work with you on your base pay, ask about flexible work hours that might improve your quality of life. Many companies are now allowing employees to work from home multiple days per week. This not only saves you time wasted in traffic but it could add up to considerable savings on your monthly fuel bills if you have a long commute. Flexible working schedules are one of the top benefits to negotiate for many people. If you feel your employer does not have any wiggle room on your compensation, this is an area that will cost them nothing to grant you and can save you a lot of time and money. It can also potentially add to a higher quality of life for you and your family. This is a massive change in the modern workplace with many companies allowing virtual work environments for their staff.

3) BENEFITS | Jobs with good benefits are becoming more difficult to find. However, you can negotiate a number of key add-ons. This will include vacation, personal time off, health care, long-term disability and life insurance, medical or disability leave, 401(k) plans with employer matching programs, and supplemental retirement benefits. If you are unable to secure the base salary you desire, ask for an extra week or two of vacation time. Many companies have a "use or lose policy" with vacation time, but if possible, request to be able to roll over unused vacation from one year to the next.

4) EQUITY COMPENSATION | As you gain more seniority, equity compensation becomes a way to incentivize experienced leaders. This is especially true of start-up company compensation packages that may not have great starting salaries but may offer equity ownership for those who help the company take hold. Depending on your company and position, you can negotiate stock options, restricted stock, and deferred compensation. Make sure you understand how and when these items vest, and how they are treated when the employment relationship ends. I highly encourage you to seek an attorney's help if possible. There are great websites out there to assist you in the negotiations. I have seen employees wooed with "stock options" only to find out years later the stock they had been granted is worthless. Anytime you have a chance to get an equity position in an established or young company, it can be a game-changer for your long-term wealth.

5) OTHER BENEFITS | Benefits such as relocation-expense payment or reimbursement, expense accounts, company car or allowance, transition assistance, an attorney, tax advice, and accountant fees for senior level leaders also play a role. All employees who are moving for a company should receive moving expenses. Don't be shy about identifying this as part of the package, and remember to negotiate a return to your home state should things end less than optimally.

6) SEVERANCE | This often-forgotten piece of compensation is critical to outline up front. Severance pay is critical for transitions and should be earned in multiple ways. First, a base severance pay can be earned for longevity. Second, it can be earned for achieved performance. Finally, if you are asked to sign a non-compete agreement, you should also work out an acceptable severance package before you sign that agreement. Commonly, employees can earn one-month severance for every year of service, and additional months can be earned for hitting specified targets.

7) DOCUMENT OWNERSHIP | The compensation agreement needs to be in writing and in your possession, signed by your direct supervisor and also a senior member of the company. Partners who are starting companies together should also have compensation agreements in place regarding cash disbursements at the end of the year and potential salaries when revenue allows it. Always make sure you retain a copy of this agreement, not just your employer. This seems basic, but I have watched hundreds of people sign contracts they could not take with them. If you are asked to do this, consider the contract worthless.

As a contractor and entrepreneur, I protect my interests with compensation agreements. I've also learned in the companies that I have led as CEO and president that great compensation agreements help motivate your team, and the things you incentivize get done.

All employers are looking for people who are trustworthy, hardworking, committed to excellence in all they do, passionate about their mission and excited to come to work, and bringing energy and enthusiasm with them each day. Steve Jobs is famous for saying to the CEO of Pepsi, who he recruited to Apple to be their new CEO, "Do you want to sell sugar the rest of your life or do you want to change the world?"[4] Don't forget, many entrepreneurs and business people want to change the world. If you do too, don't hesitate to tell them what you are passionate about and what motivates you each day. A motivated person will change the world, and companies need this excitement in their DNA. If you are this type of person and have been delivering for your organization, don't be afraid to sit down and talk about your compensation. It is only fair to be compensated for the value you bring to the company. Unless you are willing to work for free, it is up to you to schedule a time to talk about these issues. Since not everyone is motivated by monetary incentives, know what is most important to you and negotiate on those points. Do you want more flexibility in your work schedule? Do you want new challenges or to work independently on a special project? Do you want to work on a corporate social responsibility project to improve your community? Whatever it is, sit down and work out a win-win agreement with your boss. If you would like to consult with an attorney experienced in negotiating employment-related agreements, I recommend contacting Doug Janney (Doug@Janneylaw.com) in Nashville. He can answer your questions and guide you through the process and meet your specific needs.

ALTERNATE REVENUE OPPORTUNITIES

Now that you have taken steps to address your compensation at your current employment, it is time to look at new revenue streams for you. There will be some who wish to build a second revenue stream to help pay off debt, fund college for their children, or save for retirement, and they do not have the desire to leave their current work situation that they enjoy. Having this second revenue stream brings security and options for them. For others, building a second income is a necessity because they know their industry is changing and they will have to look for work soon. Some may utterly despise their job and need an escape. For those looking to make the leap, most will start as an *intrepreneur* for some time to build the skills, capital, and the business they want to start before leaving. The term *intrepreneur* started being thrown around in the mid-'90s to describe an employee at a large corporation who was given the latitude to start a project, take risks, and build something with the larger business. Basically, "intrepreneuring" allowed the employee to act like a start-up entrepreneur with the funding, resources, and safety net of the parent company.[5] Today this term is taking on a new meaning. Many people are becoming intrepreneurs while working their standard nine-to-five job that pays the bills and provides security for them, then after work they transition and pursue the creation of their start-up company—growing it to the point where they can make a shift and rely on this as their full-time calling. This intrepreneur transition period is very important. You want to be fully prepared before you cut the cord and become a full-time entrepreneur.

The entrepreneurial lifestyle is seen by many as the ideal way to intentionally engineer your life around the things you are passionate about. It gives people more control and flexibility, and the idea of being your own boss and leaving the politics of the corporate world is a dream of many.

Certain sectors of the economy are showing rapid growth in this area. Many new MBAs graduating from the top business school programs today are going into the start-up world, a big departure from the pull of Wall Street and finance careers that a few years ago pulled in most of the top aspiring graduates. Women are a growing demographic that are leading the way in entrepreneur start-ups. Three times as many women are starting new businesses as men with over 550 women starting a business each day![6] Studies show that more and more professional women who quit the workforce to start a family are not going back to the corporate world but instead are becoming entrepreneurs at a faster rate than ever as they build second income-streams for their families. They have a financial and family drive to be successful and they are setting the bar high.

Global organizations working to solve the current job crisis are looking to increase entrepreneurial programs in schools around the world to empower the next generation of entrepreneurs. They know that governments cannot create the jobs that will be needed over the next ten years and that a new generation of entrepreneurs must be taught and empowered to create the jobs of the future.

> BECOMING AN INTREPRENEUR WILL ALLOW YOU TO GROW YOUR BUSINESS SKILLS WHILE DEVELOPING YOUR SIDE BUSINESS AND INCREASING YOUR INCOME IN THE PROCESS.

For the vast majority, I recommend testing and growing your entrepreneurial skills by becoming an intrepreneur first. Launching a new venture—whether it is a small, part-time side business or a full-blown start-up company—requires a lot of hard work, intestinal fortitude, and the courage to get through days and weeks of pain while you build your dream. I personally love the start-up world because it is full of excitement and opportunity. However, the start-up process can be arduous, so it is important to do something that you are passionate about. No matter what you do, if you love it, you won't be working but will be enjoying the process. There will be moments where you have to get outside your comfort zone, but overall, doing something you love will make the process much more enjoyable.

There are many cost-effective ways to start this process to build a truly sustainable and rewarding income stream for your family. Becoming an intrepreneur will allow you to grow your business skills while developing your side business and increasing your income in the process. With the proliferation of new technology and free applications, it is easier than ever to start a side business. Here is my recommended tool kit for the start-up intrepreneur.

INTREPRENEUR / ENTREPRENEUR:
A RECOMMENDED START-UP TOOL KIT

WEBSITE AND TECHNOLOGY | Having a home base on the web is important. I prefer using GoDaddy for my domain registrations and specialized email services. Use HostGator.com to host your website and I highly recommend WordPress.com as the service you use to design your personalized website. WordPress has a robust platform with many applications to meet your needs. You can get a free theme or pay a little extra to get a special theme that has more functionality. You can view my personal website at www.RobertDickie.com. My email, Robert@RobertDickie.com, is hosted through my GoDaddy account. Both services are easy to use. Paying for a few hours to have a professional help you with some of the more difficult tasks is worth it!

FINANCE | It is becoming increasingly common to pay for services online and for payments to be received on our handheld devices. Use PayPal to receive payments for consulting services and have this linked to FreshBooks, a free online invoicing and time-tracking tool for services you provide. Sign up for a free Square account so you can take credit card transactions from your mobile devices.

MARKETING | Staying in touch with clients is important. I use MailChimp as my email service that is linked with my website. As people sign up to stay in touch with you and your company, you are able to send out mass emails to your clients informing them of updates, sales, and special promotions. I also use SendOutCards to send out personalized greeting cards on holidays to a select group of my best clients. This is a great way to add a personal touch but still have it automated so it saves some time.

YOUR PERSONAL OFFICE | I am amazed at all the free tools available today on the web. I prefer using Google for most of my business needs, so I have a Gmail account and I routinely use Google+ to communicate with clients and Google Drive and Dropbox to store many of my documents. It is amazing to have access to all your documents no matter where you are in the world. Since I do a great deal of online reading and research, I use Pocket .com to store articles that I can reference later. Many times as I am out in a coffee shop I don't have time to clip links and save them.

With Pocket loaded on my computer, I am able to hit a button any-time I am reading something online and it is "auto-magically" saved in an online folder for future reference. I have used it extensively while researching content for this book. A project management tool that I use with multiple teams around the globe is BaseCamp. This service costs a few dollars a month but is a great way to com-municate with a geographically separated group of people, share documents and calendars, and coordinate activities. Finally, since I do a lot of traveling and have many reservations for airline tickets, hotels, and rental cars, I love TripIT. This free service syncs with your email account to keep all your reservations in one place. It will give you updates on flight changes, gate changes, and delays, and upon arrival give you information on your rental car and hotel.

COMMUNICATION | Many years ago when I was in the mili-tary I remember when the video conferencing equipment was just coming out. It was very expensive and the reliability wasn't always the best. Today I use video conferencing on a daily basis with cli-ents, business partners, friends, and family all over the world and most often use Google Hangout. There are times when I have to use a traditional phone conference call and when that happens I use FreeConference.com. I love the fact that I can be in my car, at home, in a coffee shop, or out in the country while conducting business. The free agent economy is amazing!

SOCIAL | It goes without saying that no matter what you are doing today, you'd better have a deep understanding of all forms of social media and how to leverage them for your business. These are becoming basic requirements for jobs, just like understanding how to use Microsoft Word or Excel is required for many profes-sions. I use Twitter, Facebook, LinkedIn, Google+, Instagram, and YouTube on a daily basis. I go further in-depth on social media in a later chapter. Millennials . . . you guys are world-class in taking advantage of these technologies. For the older generations, just understand these are free tools you need to become proficient in using (#Important!). It is becoming increasingly common for mid-career professionals in a state of transition who are applying for a new job to not get accepted because they had no idea how to use these services. These are not just time-wasters for teenagers. Every major corporation in the country is now using all of these services and building strategies and investing millions of dollars to have these be part of their growth plan for the future.

START A HOME-BASED BUSINESS IN DIRECT SALES

"This is the last bastion of free enterprise!" exclaims Tom Chenault about the direct sales and network marketing industry. Tom is an industry icon, has his own radio show, and is always excited to share his story. "I have been covering this industry for 26 years on my show, and for those willing to invest the time, to learn, and to stay focused on their goals I think it is one of the best revenue streams you can develop. It does not come easy, but over time, with focused hard work, it can yield what many opportunities cannot." Tom's love of people and the industry runs to his core. He has built his business and career on his motto of "Love like crazy and then love some more," which has endeared him to many who flee the rat race of corporate America looking for a place where they can be appreciated and where they are not just a number in a machine but can be a part of a team trying to achieve more.

> GO OUT AND TEST THE MARKET AND SEE WHAT PEOPLE THINK OF YOUR IDEA. IF THEY ARE WILLING TO PAY YOU, YOU ARE IN BUSINESS.

The Direct Selling Association is the governing body of the direct sales and network marketing industry. In 2012, the industry did $31.6 billion in revenue with 15.9 million people in North America participating in some form of direct sales.[7] To put it in context, the National Football League brought in $9.5 billion in 2012.[8] With a wide range of companies and products to choose from and generally low barrier of entry, this type of home-based business is seen by many as a great step to build additional revenue for their family. Not surprisingly, women are entering this space faster than ever to build a second income for their family, working with companies like Pampered Chef, Avon, Mary Kay, Rodan+Fields, Matilda Jane, Thirty-One, Stella&Dot, Youngevity, Life Shotz, and Beachbody, to name a few. There is an option for almost any lifestyle. The participants seek the benefits of low cost of entry, flexible work schedules, and the ability to work out of their home. A great deal of due diligence is recommended to ensure you choose the right opportunity and sign up with a reputable company. As with any industry, there are organizations with long track records of success and those who have less-than-stellar records and give the industry a bad name. Recent legal action by the Federal Trade Commission has taken down a few egregious offenders, helping protect consumers and also strengthen the governing laws to ensure fair trade practices. If you are considering a home-based business in the direct sales industry, I recommend starting your search at the Direct Selling Association website. I also encourage anyone presented with an opportunity to check with the Better Business Bureau and even the state Attorney General's office to see if there are any issues with the business you are researching.

Those who have the greatest success in building a part-time business take their time to do their due diligence and find great opportunities that are in alignment with their values.

If starting with an established home-based business within the direct sales industry is not for you, many start by bootstrapping their own idea. My business partner Wade Myers, who founded Venture Academy, always says the best way to start a business is to get a customer. If you have an idea, there is no better way to find out if it will work than to secure your first paying customer. Go out and test the market and see what people think of your idea. If they are willing to pay you, you are in business. World-renowned English businessman and founder/chairman of the Virgin Group Richard

Branson is famous for saying, "If somebody offers you an opportunity but you are not sure you can do it, say yes—then learn how to do it later!"[9] That is great advice from someone who did the same thing when he started his successful music business in Great Britain many decades ago.

Some people will start with leveraging specific skills they have obtained in their career and begin a side business or even go into a consulting business. I have known others who have started lawn care or home care businesses that they do in the evenings and weekends that have grown to be very lucrative. These may seem like small ideas, but I have known many people who have started with a few hundred dollars of extra revenue a month and grown this into tens of thousands a month. They have been able to pay off their homes and fully fund their retirement with their side projects. Every successful side business started small. The key is to start doing something extra on the side outside of your normal job. Even adding just a few hundred extra dollars to the bottom line to a monthly budget can make a substantial difference.

BECOME A FREELANCER OR CONSULTANT

One of the best ways to build a second source of revenue is to leverage your current skills and past experience. A growing trend in the marketplace is for people to become a consultant, and with new services like FreeLancer.com it is easier than ever. There are many options for people to consider. Although the joke is that anyone who is unemployed becomes a consultant, the truth is that people around the world who value quality of life, being in control, and being intentional in lifestyle design are choosing to be freelancers because of the freedom it offers. There are those who find themselves displaced or in transition and will look to bring in temporary revenue as a consultant while they find their next long-term job, but a growing segment of the population is not using this as a transition opportunity but as their way of crafting a meaningful life based on their schedule, values, and priorities. This is an easy side revenue-stream for those in a service-based and knowledge-based environment where their skills are in demand in many industries or businesses. Using the tools mentioned previously, someone can build a very profitable consulting business in a short time frame. For some, this has been so lucrative that it ends up becoming their full-time career.

You can start your practice on your own with little to no overhead. For those considering this, I highly recommend checking out Freelancer.com. It is an industry leader with over 12 million registered users and over 6 million engagements currently being offered.[10] Not only can you advertise your skill set to prospective employers and also search engagements that are being advertised that would be a perfect fit for you, but you can use Freelancer.com to search for experts who you can pay to help launch your project or start your side business. This is a great service to test the waters and see what is out there. Nikki Parker, the Regional Director of North America and Oceania for Freelancer.com, says that "the popularity of flexible work arrangements can be seen by a global Towers Watson survey which reports that nearly half (47%) of the companies surveyed have staff working remotely or in a flexible working arrangement. This number is going to continue to grow." Nikki encourages college students to use Freelancer.com while they are in college to start building a work portfolio before they enter the job market. For those who currently have a full-time job this is a great way to start building a side business leveraging your skill sets and industry knowledge. The top five job categories on Freelancer.com are:

1. Design—Web design, logo design, creative design, etc.
2. Technology—Website, software, and application development
3. Content Creation—Report writing, research, article writing, and blog writing
4. Personal Assistants—Data entry and virtual assistants

5. Online Marketing—Search engine optimization, Facebook and Google advertising, etc.

For those who have industry experience and have been operating as a part-time consultant and are ready to operate on a larger scale, you can partner with reputable national firms who specialize in working with consultants. You may be familiar with some of the big consulting firms like McKinsey, Boston Consulting Group, and Bain & Company that regularly make the news as they work with the government and large multinational companies. Bain & Company was made famous in the last election because the investing affiliate Bain Capital was started by Republican presidential nominee Mitt Romney. These firms generally only hire the very best graduates right out of the top business schools in the country. However, a good friend of mine, Loren Bendele, the founder and current president of Savings.com, got his start in the professional world when he graduated from Texas A&M and wanted to work for the Boston Consulting Group. He called them asking for an interview and they told him they were not interviewing anyone from his school. He was just an undergraduate and they were only interviewing MBAs from the top schools in the country. Undeterred, Loren let them know he was a chemical engineer with great grades and 15 months of experience with Dow Chemical. He told them he would pay his way and fly to Boston to get the chance to interview. Loren took the leap and they loved his tenacity. At the end of the interview they told him he had done better than all the MBAs. He got the job and it proved to be a pivotal role in his career that later helped him found Savings.com in Los Angeles. (Note: Loren took action and was committed to his plan and it paid off!)

Many well-known placement and temporary-employment companies have built departments around providing "consultant services" for their corporate clients who need to hire industry experts for a temporary project. Firms like Diag Partners, VACO,

Robert Half, and Grant Thornton seek out professionals who have expert industry knowledge and want to work as consultants in a specialized niche. The benefit of working with a placement firm like these is they will be working to market you to all their clients and seeking out new business opportunities for you. In effect, they will keep your pipeline full, so once you complete an engagement you have another one waiting for you. For their services, firms like this will collect up to 50 percent of your billing rate. The upside is you get to work with a national brand, use their resources, and have them continue to market you and your services while you are working with clients.

Katie King, a former VACO executive who recently transitioned to Grant Thornton, says these firms love professional consultants they can work with because they are looking for recurring revenue streams for their businesses and a great consultant can bring this in for them month after month. Her advice is to always take care of your consulting firm, because if you do a great job for their client, your firm will work hard to keep you busy. You in effect are generating a great deal of revenue for them and if they don't keep you busy you could get picked up by a marketplace competitor and start working on a project for them.

KNOW WHAT YOU ARE AN EXPERT IN AND THEN SPEND TIME MARKETING YOURSELF AROUND THAT NICHE.

If you decide to work independently, you will get to collect 100 percent of your billing rate. However, you will not have the benefits of working with a national brand and have a team of people market you and your services. If you don't want to have breaks in activity, Katie recommends that you continuously work on your pipeline. No matter what you are doing, spend some time each day working on new leads and preparing your next client. Katie also recommends that the sole practitioner understand the tax differences between being a W-2 employee and a 1099 contractor. As you start to build your practice, it is critical to get some expert help in this area so you do not make a mistake with the IRS. It is up to you to withhold proper taxes and remit those to the IRS.

Finally, the successful consultant will become a specialist in a niche and exploit it. It has been said, "Riches are in niches," and this is true in the consultant world. Being a generalist is too vague and wide open, and potential clients will not lead to lucrative business. Know what you are an expert in and then spend time marketing yourself around that niche. Plug yourself into the industry and make sure to attend the right conferences and social events. Get out and be social. Your network is the most important marketing tool to grow your consulting practice and secure engagements. Network, network, network! This is a relevant theme throughout this book. I asked Katie for some parting advice to those navigating this new economy and securing employment to have a successful career. Without hesitation she said, "Networking is everything! You have to be networking at all times. Be connected, be social, and understand your contacts are your game changer!"

BUY A FRANCHISE

If someone has considerable savings or access to capital, one way to make the leap into entrepreneurship has been to buy a national franchise that comes with a proven system, but this can be costly. The investment can be anywhere from $40,000 to $3.5M depending on the business. Generally these are proven systems that can generate great income over time if you execute the plan properly. If you have money to invest *and* have industry knowledge this might be an option for you. There are many websites and advisors to help you investigate and research national franchises if this is a route you are looking to explore. I would start with SBA.org and Entrepreneur .com. A great deal of due diligence is required to ensure you are investing in the right business with a proven track record and support system. If you are looking to buy a franchise, start your research with the Federal Trade Commission, which regulates this industry.

Recently, I heard a presentation where a gentleman told a story of his friend who had worked as a consultant for a well-known convenience store chain for many years and decided he wanted to open his own store. The two started to investigate what it would cost to buy a franchise store. Here is what they discovered.

- The franchise fee to start was $300K
- To build a store in a great location would cost $2 million
- An average store earns on average $500K a year
- $250K goes back to the franchise and the owner keeps $250K
- After tax, the owner might clear $150K a year[11]

It did not take long to see that this was not an opportunity that was right for them. His friend would be starting with $2.3 million in debt with 50 percent of their profits going to the franchise. With meager profits and a massive debt payment it would take years to get back to even.

Many times when you are considering taking on debt to launch a business various forms for partnerships come into play. A partner might bring experience and industry knowledge to the table and they might also be needed to help fund the operation by bringing capital. A partnership in business is like a marriage. Choose wisely! A business divorce is extremely painful and messy.

THE START-UP GAME IS A CHALLENGING ENVIRONMENT AND FRAUGHT WITH OBSTACLES; IT IS NOT FOR THE WEAK OF HEART.

For those who are ready to raise funding for your new business idea, you can start today. In the past, you had to seek out angel investors to get you started, and they would take part ownership of your company. Today you can crowd-source with these great sites and still retain 100 percent ownership of your site. Some people have raised a few thousand dollars, while others have raised hundreds of thousands and even over a million dollars for their businesses with these sites.

- Kickstarter.com
- Indiegogo.com
- GoFundMe.com

If you are launching a new business, watch the Venture Academy Videos at Crownbiz.com to help you avoid common pitfalls and put your idea for success on the fast track.

The start-up game is a challenging environment and fraught with obstacles; it is not for the weak of heart. When speaking with people in the midst of their start-up, you will generally hear two tales. One is of the excitement and passion for their product/service, the joy of being in control, being their own boss, and charting their course in the world. The other tale is of the hard work, long hours, doubts, financial stress, questioning if they made a mistake, wondering when they will turn the corner and have their first big success and how much longer can they afford to go. Everyone in the start-up game will have both tales to tell and you might experience both in the same day. It is exhilarating and terrifying, with bursts of passionate, focused energy combined with mentally and physically exhausting stretches when you wonder if you should give up.

IF YOU ARE STARTING A BUSINESS THAT INVOLVES A PARTNERSHIP, THIS IS THE MOST IMPORTANT THING TO GET RIGHT.

If you are still passionate about starting your business, you need to first address the issues that are most likely to hinder your success. The Small Business Administration reports that only 44 percent of businesses started will survive to the fourth year.[12] The SBA, who underwrites more small business loans than any organization in the United States, lists the top three reasons for start-up failures as: lack of experience, lack of capital, and poor location.[13] Much has been written about these issues so I would like to highlight three seldom discussed issues that can torpedo your start-up. There are plenty of obstacles that an entrepreneur must face when launching their business but the worst ones tend to be self-inflicted. If you avoid these mistakes you will have an exponentially greater chance for success.

POOR PARTNERS | According to Marquette University Kohler Center for Entrepreneurship, "More than 90% of America's fastest growing companies are partnerships."[14] Starting a company with partners that bring multiple skill sets and abilities to the table is a proven winner. However, starting a company with partners that have misaligned values, inconsistent outcome expectations, or a lack of trust is a killer. I have experienced this firsthand and have watched multiple companies unravel and sometimes never launch due to poor partner relationships. If you are starting a business that involves a partnership, this is the most important thing to get right. If you get this wrong, I believe your company will have no chance for success until it is fixed. In his bestselling book *The Speed of Trust*, Stephen Covey chronicles why this is so important. Make sure you trust your partner, your values are aligned, your roles are clearly defined, and there is total alignment of future expectations. Do you both want to look for a sale and exit in three to five years or do you want to build a family company that you can pass on to your children?

DELAYED LAUNCH | Planning is a critical process to have success. We have all heard that if you don't have a plan you are planning to fail. However, I have seen too many start-ups stay too long in the discussion, white-board, dreaming stage with a failure to launch. Seth Godin implores young entrepreneurs to just "ship it." It doesn't have to be perfect, but get started and quickly iterate as you get customer feedback. Eric Ries, an entrepreneur in residence at Harvard Business School and the author of *The Lean Startup*, encourages entrepreneurs to "launch with a minimum viable product," see how the market responds, and quickly make changes and improvements accordingly.[15] Too much time thinking about ideas, planning, and over-analyzing will allow competitors to take the first-mover advantage. One of my Harvard Business School professors once said in a lecture, "Remember that if you have an idea there are probably at least ten other people in the world thinking about the same thing. He who launches first generally wins." Be wise and make plans as you launch your business but launch as quickly as you can and make improvements with your customers' feedback and support. Richard Branson summed it up best when he said, "You don't learn to walk by following rules. You learn by doing and falling over."[16]

LACK OF STRATEGIC FOCUS | We have seen large corporations like HP lose market share due to lack of focus. A lack of strategic focus for a small start-up has the same disastrous consequences. Understanding your industry, local market, and competitive advantage is the key to success. Trying to be all things to all people is a recipe for disaster. For example, Taco Bell knows what its strategic focus is . . . they are simply a low-cost Mexican fast-food restaurant. How bizarre would it be to walk into a Taco Bell and find them selling burgers and $40 Mexican entrees? Far too often start-up entrepreneurs don't know how to say NO. Not every sale is a good sale and not every customer is a good customer. Knowing how to say no to certain customers and staying focused with your core target audience that knows and appreciates you and what you offer is essential. My father told me that the surest way to failure is to try to please everyone. Learn about your industry and customers, have a true understanding of your unique abilities, develop a strategic focus around that, and say no to the rest. By not being distracted with other opportunities you will have the greatest success. Simon Sinek, the author of the *New York Times* bestselling book *Start With Why,* and whose TED Talk of the same title has also become one of the most watched TED Talks of all time, says, "The goal of business then should not be to simply sell to anyone who wants what you have, but rather to find people who believe what you believe."[17] Find those people, take care of them, and you will have a successful business.

I have started multiple businesses, operated two, and consulted with many more and each one has provided its own unique excitement and challenges. The start-up environment is my favorite. If you are passionate about your idea, seek advice and counsel from trusted mentors in your life and start your venture. I am sure you will soon say, "Why didn't I take the leap earlier?"

I HAVE HEARD MULTIPLE ENTREPRENEURS SAY THEY LEARNED MORE FOUNDING AND RUNNING THEIR START-UP BUSINESS THAN THEY DID GETTING THEIR MBA.

The old adage of digging your well before you are thirsty is more applicable now than ever. The great thing is that you have more free tools than ever before. You really have all the resources you need to launch your side project. Since it takes time and effort to get it set up, I encourage you to start today. If you don't have a plan, start developing one, and take little action steps each day to make progress on this goal. There are plenty of options. Choose something you are passionate about and this will be a fun hobby for you and not just another job. The process of building your plan and putting all the pieces of the puzzle together will be a first-class education that will help you in your current job. I have heard multiple entrepreneurs say they learned more founding and running their start-up business than they did getting their MBA. Life has a way of teaching us what a classroom cannot and this real-life experience will be a great asset to have. Furthermore, if you lose your job in the future, you will be glad to have a second source of income. If you never have to go through the pain of losing a job but over time build a second revenue stream that eventually produces a solid income for your family, this could fund your retirement and savings accounts 100 percent. This is a great rainy-day fund and it gives you many options, which are always nice to have.

Starting a business is always hard. It will take enormous amounts of work and many times up-front investments in "sweat equity" and capital. The best advice I can give is to make sure you are *passionate* about what you are doing. If you are, you will enjoy the journey more and you will be able to get through the rough spots. Here are some websites that will help you get started if you decide to work as a freelancer or start up a part-time business.

- TaskRabbit.com
- Freelancer.com
- Gigwalk.com
- Elance.com
- Etsy.com
- Guru.com

For those launching a part-time business as a freelancer who are worried about health, dental, and disability insurance, along with how to continue with your life insurance and retirement planning, check out FreelancersUnion.org on how to join the growing group of 42 million freelancers in America who range from nannies to lawyers and are working on solutions.

We are entering the most insecure job market of the past century. Global unemployment is rising, with the demand for jobs increasing daily. As global economies struggle to create jobs for the growing workforce, the pressure increases daily. In Asia alone, one million new people enter the job market each month needing employment! In America, we have unfunded retirement plans and corporations facing increasing pressure with decreasing margins. These companies continue to look at ways to decrease overhead and cut jobs, pensions, and health care responsibilities. The best thing anyone can do in this economy is to take matters into their own hands. Reduce your debt, save for your freedom fund, and build a passive income stream that will be there for you in retirement. You don't want to start thinking about this when you are 65.

LEAPING BY EXAMPLE

BUILDING YOUR INCOME: Anne Beiler, *Auntie Anne's Pretzels, founder and former CEO*

"People too often focus on what they don't have instead of what they do have and that becomes their greatest obstacle. It was for me. I had an eighth-grade education, and I was so intimidated by those who had more education and money than me. I was letting that hold me back. When I overcame that my business took off." Anne Beiler was born in Lancaster County, Pennsylvania, in 1949 in an Amish Mennonite background. Armed with an eighth-grade education and a farm-raised, strong work ethic and sheer determination, she started a pretzel business in Downington, Pennsylvania. She admits her first pretzels were horrible, but that was not her biggest obstacle.

Her self-doubt and continued focus on the things she did not have kept her from seeing her potential and the things she was blessed with. "Finally, one day my husband told me to change my focus. When I sat down and looked at it, I had far more than I thought. I had a purpose! I wanted to give back to the world. I had a great product and I worked with great people. That is when everything changed for me." The growth of Auntie Anne's Pretzels took off. "Many times we find our purpose in the pain in our life. People need to understand that. I tell people to focus on the three small p's: purpose, product, and people. If you do this consistently well, it will give you the capital P that every business needs to thrive in business and that is PROFIT." As the company continued to grow, the greatest challenge became the art of delegation. "Many entrepreneurs want to be in charge of everything. I was no different. I had to learn to let go and let other people take control. Delegation becomes essential for growth and I would encourage all young entrepreneurs to learn this early in their career."

Her final advice: "I have heard it said many times, an entrepreneur is one who is willing to work 16 hours a day so they don't have to work eight for someone else. If you are not willing to work those hours, don't start. Being an entrepreneur is like owning a farm. It is 24 hours a day, seven days a week, 365 days a year. It requires hard work. The other thing I would say is that the greatest reward wasn't the income that gave me the life I had dreamed of. That was nice, but the *real* reward was helping others, giving people a great place to work, helping families that were struggling, being a good boss, and caring for my employees. I was able to see people grow personally and professionally. People's lives were changed. That was the greatest joy! We don't truly begin to live until we learn to give."

Auntie Anne's Pretzels continued to grow at a rapid pace. Anne Beiler sold the company in 2005 so she and her husband could focus all their time in counseling others. Anne's franchise soon went global, and in 2006 the one billionth pretzel was sold. In 2008 Anne was asked to deliver a speech at the Republican National Convention. Not bad for a doubting farm girl with an eighth-grade education.

STICKING THE LANDING

- With your advisor, analyze your Career Direct® assessment along with your work history and resume to where you have areas of expertise ready to be leveraged for second sources of income. Are you best suited to get a part-time job, become a freelancer, consultant, or start your own business?

- Create an action plan to increase your income over the next one, three, and five years with revenue goals. Where will that extra income be placed? Will it go to pay down debt, save for retirement, etc.?

- If you have a business opportunity you are considering launching, go to OpportunityIQ.com to run an analysis on it before you invest your money and time. Created by Wade Myers while he was at the Boston Consulting Group, this process analyzes over 50 principles of a business to provide a detailed report on your opportunity. This has been done on thousands of businesses and it will let you know whether your idea has a high probability for success.

CHAPTER 6

BUILD YOUR BRAND

"Remember that your reputation is everything. You build your personal brand through everything you do, whether big actions or small decisions, and that brand will stay with you throughout your career."

—JAN FIELDS

Most people have an emotional connection with a brand that deeply resonates with them for some unknown reason. Others become so committed to a brand, they are known by industry insiders as "brand evangelists." They talk about the brand and its products or services almost like they are having a deeply spiritual moment. Great brands are simple and tap into your emotions. They leave a lasting mark and many people are loyal to their brands until the day they die. Simply put, brands matter to people.

For example, think about Nike, BMW, and Apple. They have spent billions building their global brand, and you never see a BMW commercial that says, "We are about cars." The successful brands have messages that go deeper and connect at an emotional level. *Just do it! The ultimate driving machine! Think different!* These are simple yet powerful slogans that reinforce the brand and craft a mental framework that defines the user experience. Just as a brand can bring great value to a company, your brand is an extremely valuable part of the equation for your success in the new part-time economy. Mary Jesse, CEO of IvyCorp, says, "A personal brand is more than what you wear. Your brand is your public identity."[1] Therefore, our goal is to understand our personal brand as well as how to build, protect, and leverage it.

PEOPLE WHO HAVE CRAFTED A GREAT PERSONAL BRAND ARE ALWAYS IN DEMAND.

Building and protecting your personal brand is extremely important in this part-time economy where a new form of free agent will craft part-time work, short-term gigs, and freelance assignments into meaningful engagements that will translate into a career over a lifetime. This is the new normal. Having a strong personal brand is essential during transitions and will be your calling card that precedes you, opening doors of opportunity even when you are not looking. For freelancers, it will keep the pipeline of projects full as clients line up to secure your services. People who have crafted a great personal brand are always in demand.

There are some people who just don't seem to get it as they are ingrained in the rules of the past and continue to work in the old economy. They think that because no one used to openly speak about personal branding it did not exist . . . but it did. What do you think of when you hear the names Frank Sinatra, John F. Kennedy, and Winston Churchill? They may not have set out to do it but they all developed powerful and lasting personal brands.

Both of my grandfathers have a personal brand that lives on today, even many years after their deaths. My paternal grandfather worked for General Motors his entire life on the factory floor and is remembered for his toughness and stoic demeanor in adversity. He would not drive any vehicle that was not a General Motors. He could have passed as John Wayne with his rough-hewn look, and to this day I remember his strong, calloused hands. Although tough, he was kind to everyone he met and is remembered for his tenacious work ethic and honesty. My maternal grandfather was a traveling evangelist in the deep South. His Southern-gentleman upbringing helped soften his stern German roots. I recall watching him deliver a passionate message as a youngster and watching his emotion overflow as the Spirit filled the church. He was known as a man on fire for Christ who was completely all-in for the cause. Over a lifetime, both men crafted a personal brand and legacy that continues to live long after their deaths. Each day we wake we are crafting our own brand and legacy that will one day outlive us.

I've had conversations with people who didn't understand this concept and thought that only companies have brands but people do not. Somewhere in the conversation they will say they don't have a personal brand or need one. I will always emphatically explain, "You already have a personal brand, you just don't know it." Your brand is simply an extension of your reputation and your character.

Building a personal brand is important and each one of us is doing it daily whether we know it or not. The question is whether your brand is helping or hurting you. During a conversation with Jerry Bostelman, CEO of VACO—one of the largest and fastest-growing placement agencies in the United States—he told me they review every potential recruit's social media accounts in depth. The college guy who posted his drunken fraternity exploits on Facebook just branded himself. If he is looking to get hired by MTV, maybe that will help him. If he is trying to land a job at Bain or Goldman Sachs, he probably won't get an interview. Your brand is important and building and protecting it is critical for success.

First you need to determine what your brand is currently. To learn about this, look no further than your contacts and various relationships. Starting with the people you know best and moving outward to get a wide variety of people, send them an email and ask them to tell you the first three things they think when they hear your name. Let them know you are doing a project and their honest answer will help you as you are trying to understand your public brand. As you read over the answers, you should start to get a general theme. If you have answers all over the place, that is okay. It just lets you know that with some intentional action you can start to craft a personal brand that will resonate with everyone you know. For example, if I say *John Maxwell*, most people will think *leadership*. If I say *Seth Godin*, most would think *marketing*. If I say *Andy Stanley*, most would think *pastor*. All three have spent considerable time honing their skills, living out their passions, and branding themselves. You can build a similar brand, but you need to know where you are starting.

Next you need to know what you want your brand to do. Where do you want to be in 5, 10, 20 years from now, and how do you plan to leverage your brand to get there? Understanding this also helps you understand your target audience. These are key steps to taking intentional action in crafting your brand. Once you know this you can create your plan with the following steps.

"KNOW THYSELF" —SOCRATES

Once you know what your current brand is and where you want to go, the next step in crafting your brand is to know who you are. What are your strengths, talents, and skills? In what area are you an expert? You want to leverage your strengths. If you have never taken a personal assessment, I recommend Crown's Personality ID® to start. And for an in-depth understanding of your skills and values, you can take a Career Direct® assessment with a trained consultant. This is a great first step to truly understanding your skill sets, passions, strengths, and weaknesses. What makes you different and unique? These are things that you want to leverage in your brand. Using the information you have discovered about yourself—like what makes you unique and different, what are your special skills and talents, what do you stand for, and what is your value proposition for others—you will be able to craft a statement that represents your brand.

AUTHENTICITY RULES

Charles Swindoll gave great advice when he said, "I know of nothing more valuable, when it comes to the all-important virtue of authenticity, than simply being who you are."[2] Plain and simple, don't try to be someone you are not. We are talking about building our personal brands for career purposes. There is no point in crafting a false reality that you cannot measure up to once you receive a job offer or freelance work. I have heard people say, "Fake it till you make it," and in this area it would be a big mistake. That type of mindset creates misalignment in life, and misalignment creates problems. Even if you have everyone fooled but yourself, you will not be happy or able to perform to your maximum potential if you are living a lie. I don't need to belabor this point. It's simple to understand and critically important to get right.

> **SOCIAL MEDIA IS THE BEST PLACE TO BUILD AND LEVERAGE YOUR BRAND.**

RELATIONSHIPS MATTER

Social media is the best place to build and leverage your brand. Many people are misinformed by thinking that social media is just about "me." Social media has always focused on connection. The foundation is about building relationships. For the novice, it is about "me," but for brand-builders it is always about "we." Your social media accounts from Facebook, LinkedIn, Twitter, Instagram, and others should be used to give your connections an authentic view of who you are—your successes, failures, joys, sorrows, passions, and fulfilling moments in life. If you are able to tap into your emotions and then reach the emotions of the reader, you will have succeeded. Each social media platform should be used differently to reach your audience with specific intent. I use Facebook to communicate with friends and family, Twitter to communicate with the world, LinkedIn to communicate with business contacts, and Instagram and Vine as an unfiltered window into my life. My blog on the other hand is a way to engage and debate with people who are passionate about the same subject matter as me but who may have different experiences and opinions.

Social media can be used to build and extend your brand, but remember that social media is always about communication, connectedness, and relationships, which we will talk about in the next chapter more in detail. Focus on building relationships while refining your brand.

WHY SHOULD I CARE?

A mentor of mine was helping me craft a brand for a company when he asked me, "Why should I care?" It immediately clarified the objective in my mind. It was not about the story I wanted to tell, but rather what was in it for the customer. Could the company solve their problem? As you craft your brand, especially if you plan to leverage this to gain employment, you need to answer the question, Why should they hire you? The ultimate objective in building your brand is to show your skills and talents and help you stand out from the crowd. You need to clearly articulate what you stand for, what you can do, and how you can help them. This will take time, and it will be different for each individual. This is the secret of building your brand. It is equal parts science and art, and it takes time to perfect it.

MASTER YOUR TRADE

Developing your brand and finding your niche is great, but remember you also need to be able to deliver the goods. When going through an intensive branding exercise with CSK Group out of Colorado Springs, founder Steve Maegdlin told our team, "Always remember your *brand promise*. This is what you promise to deliver to our customers and supporters each day. Never deviate from that, and always deliver!" This was great advice, and it holds true in personal branding. Become a master at your trade, and always deliver to your customers. If you don't, you won't have a prominent brand any longer, and your opportunities will dry up. Mastering your trade and delivering on your brand promise is the best way to protect and build your brand.

EVOLVE

Over time you may find that your direction in life changes or your goals and passions might slightly change. It is possible and even okay to pivot and alter your brand to reflect these changes. The best example of this is Michael Hyatt, the former CEO of Thomas Nelson in Nashville. He has crafted one of the best personal brands, and I consider him an expert on personal branding. He is so good that he has developed his own theme on WordPress called "GetNoticed." Of all the themes I've studied I consider it the most user-friendly, so I use it for my personal theme for my blog. You can listen to the weekly podcast *This Is Your Life with Michael Hyatt* to get more great information on personal branding. Michael notes that through his career he has evolved over time and thus his personal brand has also changed as he has transitioned from various passion projects he was writing about. Don't be afraid to change your personal brand as well.

TOOLS TO USE

I encourage you to have a spot on the Internet that is your home where you can start to craft your online identity. This is different from all your other social media outlets. My blog is www.RobertDickie.com, and as I said before, I have this hosted with GoDaddy, which also offers email service. I recommend using an email like this that is an extension of your blog. Why? First of all, a branded email looks more professional than one from a free service like AOL or Yahoo. Second, this will help you drive more traffic to your blog and the content you are creating. Depending on your goals, you can start to publish your own content, create your own podcast, and publically speak on the niche you are an expert in. Over time, with intentional effort, you will be building a powerful personal brand.

YOUR RESUME: AN EXTENSION OF YOUR BRAND

Your resume is an extension of your personal brand, and today there are seminars on how to craft the best resume possible with the right key words, industry jargon, and fluffy self-praise. However, as it turns out in our socially minded society, a change is taking place. As companies grow in their corporate social responsibility efforts in the community, they are starting to want to see similar community activism and "giving back" in the applicants they hire. Have you ever wondered what Jesus would like to see on a resume? It turns out that His shortlist is important to employers as well. Topping the list is a willingness to work hard and a commitment to developing your spiritual gifts and talents. "All hard work brings a profit, but mere talk leads only to poverty," notes Proverbs 14:23, and also, "Lazy hands make for poverty, but diligent hands bring wealth" (Proverbs 10:4).

No one wants an employee who is more interested in the benefits than what is expected of them on the job. Especially as the cost of developing an employee is on the rise, finding someone who takes the job seriously, will be a good fit, and will provide value to the company is more important than ever. Those on the job should remember Jesus gave an entreaty to work while it is still day (John 9:4). One way to cut through the pack is to illustrate your willingness to work hard through your track record of going the extra mile to achieve a job well done.

Another important factor in evaluating someone's character related to work is how seriously a potential employee takes the development of the skills and talents they uniquely possess. The apostle Paul wrote, "Do your best to present yourself to God as one approved, a worker who does not need to be ashamed and who correctly handles the word of truth" (2 Timothy 2:15).

And it will pay off. Proverbs 22:29 observes: "Do you see someone skilled in their work? They will serve before kings; they will not serve before officials of low rank." No matter how tight the job market, there is always a competition for the most talented individuals.

However, it turns out that charitable efforts, volunteerism, and an eye toward needs in the community make the list of things that were important to Jesus.

Consider the resume and commendation of the Proverbs 31 woman, an entrepreneur and working mother: "She opens her arms to the poor and extends her hands to the needy" (v. 20). Even today, companies are looking for people who don't just give lip service to the company's reputation but are excited to get involved and make the world a better place. Multiple search firm executives said that this is becoming important not only for companies but also for the leaders doing the hiring.

> WE CAN HAVE ALL THE BUZZWORDS OF THE DAY ON OUR RESUME AND ALL THE EDUCATION TO SET US APART FROM THE REST, BUT IF WE DO ALL THIS FOR PERSONAL GAIN, IT WILL BE FOR NOTHING.

In talking about the ultimate job review, Jesus detailed in Matthew 25 the personal concern He wants people to show for others, especially the least among us. He asked people to be practical and personal in their concern for others. Jesus didn't write a check or give a donation to an organization. He got down on His hands and knees and served the sick and dying. He got dirty as He served. He didn't ask someone else to do it, He was involved in serving, and He asks us to do the same. A donation does not check off this box.

Jesus also said, "For I was hungry and you gave me something to eat, I was thirsty and you gave me something to drink, I was a stranger and you invited me in; I needed clothes and you clothed me, I was sick and you looked after me, I was in prison and you came to visit me" (Matthew 25:35–36). He thanked those for caring for Him and He calls us to do the same for those in our midst, in our neighborhoods and cities. This is what He wants us to be. This is what He wants us to represent. We can have all the buzzwords of the day on our resume and all the education to set us apart from the rest, but if we do all this for personal gain, it will be for nothing. Christ calls us to be better, to set the example, and to use all the talents He has given us to help those in need.

A willingness to share your resources, time, and talent with others has benefits in the workplace, in part because a person who looks to help others represents the kind of employee who builds up a team, sacrifices for the greater good, and does not see self-aggrandizement alone as the only goal of a career. That kind of team spirit builds up a workplace. "A generous person will prosper; whoever refreshes others will be refreshed," notes Proverbs 11:25.

Recently, Crown did a survey of business leaders asking how important community service and volunteering was to them in evaluating potential employees. Fifty percent said they always checked to see whether potential employees were engaged in volunteering, while 7 out of 10 said it was often important in deciding between qualified candidates.

Frustrating as it may be for job seekers, it's a buyer's market out there for employers, leaving them with many options when it comes to hiring. In fact, 20 percent of us live in a family in which no one has a job, according to the Bureau of Labor Statistics. However, that doesn't mean these people don't want a job.[3]

For those seeking a career and not just a job, perhaps the best way toward this objective begins with putting others' needs first. Consider the volunteer and community service opportunities around you, using your time to help those less fortunate, and showing potential employers that the content of your character makes you the right person for the job. Napoleon Hill said, "It is literally true that you can succeed best and quickest by helping others succeed."[4]

BRINGING IT HOME

Building your personal brand is not something you can accomplish over a weekend, but you can get a good start making a plan, taking stock of where you are and where you want to go, updating your social media accounts, and launching a blog. It can take years to build a strong personal brand, and the most important work will be done as you live your life and engage with those around you. Every encounter, business relationship, and transaction is a small part of building your brand. Just like corporate brands, it can be ruined overnight by one bad decision. We all can think of sports figures, politicians, or business leaders who once had stellar personal brands only to have these forever damaged due to scandals. The public is generally willing to forgive, but those brands will never be the same. Be wise in protecting your brand and don't do anything that would not be in alignment with your brand values.

LEAPING BY EXAMPLE

BUILD YOUR BRAND: Kirk Cameron, *actor, director, producer*

"I can sum up my brand with two words: *faith* and *family*." Kirk Cameron has built and leveraged his personal brand to become a prolific actor, director, and producer—working with films like *Fireproof* (the highest-grossing independent film in 2008), *Monumental, Unstoppable, Mercy Rule*, and now a three-film contract with Sony's Provident Films.

"I have to admit I had a leg up in building my brand. I started acting at the age of nine and by 14 was a star on *Growing Pains*, which became a big deal. By 19 that was how I had spent the majority of my life. I had this great platform, but in reality I wanted to be a doctor. However, when I met the girl of my dreams and wanted to get married, I knew I couldn't go back to school and then do medical school. I needed to work and make a living, and acting was all I knew. I looked at my resources, and the train had kind of left the station, so I had to seize the opportunity God had given me.

"I realized I had to go out and blaze a trail. I was not getting any phone calls from Stephen Spielberg, so eventually you have to get off the couch and make things happen," Kirk joked. "I started with a film called *The Way of the Master*, which opened the door for me to be asked to participate in *Fireproof*. But even after the great success of *Fireproof*, no one was calling me with job offers. I realized I was sitting on top of an amazing opportunity, and I had to just go out and work hard and make things happen."

Kirk's faith and values had always been an important part of his life, but this was when he started to intentionally ask the question, "What does the church culture want?" Since then, all of his work has revolved around the theme of "faith and family." "I try to embody this in all I do," he said. "If you are going to build a brand you have to be all in. You can't be a part-time actor, golfer, counselor, etc. You have to know what you are good at and passionate about and then be an expert there. Once you become an expert, use it to serve and help other people. That is when you will become successful."

His advice for leapers? "Don't wait for other people to take care of you! Your success and your opportunities will come from *your* hard work and drive. Try to develop a team and bring talented people together to accomplish your mission. You help them and they help you, and everyone wins together."

Kirk also poignantly stated, "Some people say that I ruined my career because I started doing family and faith–based films. I was following my personal values and my faith. I needed to be true to myself above all else. I would have fallen off the map had I not done that. My career would be over. I was just being true to my core principles, and God has blessed me for that. It is important for people to understand that."

As you build your brand and life, remember Kirk's story and brand yourself in a way that is in alignment with who you are and your value system.

STICKING THE LANDING

- Ask five business associates this simple question: "When you hear my name, what are the first things that come to mind? Please write two or three sentences that describe your thoughts and most importantly your feelings and emotions when you think of me." Put these comments down in a Word document in paragraph form. This will give you the beginnings of your current personal brand.

- If you like what you are reading, the next step is to play to your strengths and expand on those areas. You can also work on weak areas over time. If you are not happy with your results, you can revector as well. Your brand goals should be in alignment with your life plan and goals.

- If you would like to research a few people who I think have done a great job building and leveraging a personal brand, look to Michael Hyatt, Marissa Mayer, Seth Godin, Andy Stanley, and Oprah Winfrey. These people are authentic. They know what they stand for, they know their strengths, and they leverage their brand and build on it daily.

- As you start to build your brand don't try to appeal to everyone. Understand who you are and what you are passionate about. It has been said, "Riches are in niches." What is your niche? Focus on your area of expertise and passion and build your brand around providing information and value in that one area.

CHAPTER 7

UTILIZE SOCIAL MEDIA

*"It takes 20 years to build a reputation and five minutes to ruin it.
If you think about that, you'll do things differently."*
—WARREN BUFFETT

I recently gave a presentation in South Africa to local businessmen, and one of the points was how to use and leverage social media in business. One gentleman running a very large company laughed and said, "Come on, social media is something my teenage girls use. It isn't for business." This is a common misconception for many older business executives. I looked him square in the eyes and told him he needed to change his paradigm and start seeing all forms of social media as business tools just as important as Microsoft Word, Excel, QuickBooks, and any other technology he is using to run his business. Social media has totally changed the landscape of marketing and how customers interact with each other and their favorite brands. It has also radically changed how companies search for, prequalify, and hire employees. If your social media gives the wrong impression, you won't even get an interview, let alone the job.

I hear many young people say that social media is just a method of communication with friends, a part of their private life, and has nothing to do with their career. Those statements are equally as wrong as this man's statement that social media is solely for teenage girls.

SOCIAL MEDIA IS NOT JUST ABOUT COMMUNICATING WITH FRIENDS AND IT CERTAINLY ISN'T PRIVATE.

A close friend of mine is the CEO of a major recruitment firm in the United States. I asked him how he searches for prospects and then does due diligence on them when filling a critical job position for a large company. Without hesitation he said that 75 percent of online searches for prospects start with LinkedIn. Once a candidate has been found, the online search moves to Facebook and Twitter to "research" the candidate to make sure he or she would be the right fit for the company. Remember, his firm is looking for people to fill a specific role. If they select you they will coach you, help you work on your resume, and then present you to the company as one of their recommendations for this position. They receive a handsome commission if they place you and they could also lose their credibility if a candidate fails to impress, so they are very invested in making sure they pick the right people that have the best chance to get hired. So if you think those crazy spring break photos or frat party pictures can't hurt your career . . . guess again. These recruiters will only put their name and reputation on the line for the very best candidates.

Social media is not just about communicating with friends and it certainly isn't private. Everything you do on social media is branding you and affecting your career success. My advice to you is to treat it like a business tool and act as if your current employer and future employer are monitoring everything . . . because they very well might be.

Leveraging social media to land your next job isn't complicated when you understand the ecosystem and have a game plan. Let's start with a visual. When you go to a job interview, whether you are a man or woman, you will generally plan what you are going to wear in advance and ensure your outfit is coordinated from your shoes, pants, shirt, jacket, and even your accessories, right? Everything works together. Think of the Hollywood red-carpet events like the Oscars and how the women and men create the image they want to portray, and everything is coordinated to get the right message across. Social media is the same. You need to have a coordinated effort bringing all the various pieces of the puzzle together to give a complete picture of you and your "brand."

Each of us has probably witnessed some form of outfit disaster in our lifetime. Lady Gaga has built a reputation on crazy outfits that draw attention to her but everyone would agree this only works for a handful of people in a very specific entertainment position. That outfit would certainly not land her a job at her local bank or investment firm.

We know that a person mixing and matching different items without regard to style and function comes off looking ridiculous. Most often this is not a person who we would lend a lot of credibility to. A social media strategy that is not planned and monitored can give this type of look and feel to a prospective employer who might be looking at you. This is not the image you want them to have. If you are trying out for the show *Radical Youth* on MTV, maybe that approach will work. If you are trying to get a real job in the real world it most certainly will hurt you.

To leverage social media, you need to start with the basics such as creating a LinkedIn account and then moving to Facebook, Twitter, and YouTube. Most people probably already have these accounts established. What we want are accounts that will *help* you land a job, and not hurt you. We may need to do a little TLC and cleanup to get those sites presentable. Remember, we want to present the best version of you. It's time to dress up in your Sunday best. These are the major platforms that will be the first search for placement firms and employers. If you have a strategy for these platforms, you are off to a great start.

First, everything in online recruitment revolves around LinkedIn. You need to have a fully developed account. LinkedIn does a great job with a status bar that shows how complete your profile is. Know this: It would be better to have no account than to have a half-done, poorly managed account. Once you start, take the time to finish it. Remember, this is your online resume. You will need the following:

• PICTURE | You need a high-resolution photo of yourself in a professional setting. This should be a head and shoulder shot. No goofy photos or distant pictures. Let people see those pearly whites. Smiles sell!

• COMPLETE BIO | In the summary section you should give a well-written review of your background and work history. If you are fresh out of college, list any full- or part-time jobs you have had in the past, organizations you have been a part of, internships, etc. This is an area where you want to list "key words" that will show up in searches that placement firms will be doing. You want to list job titles, certifications, and any key word that helps describe you and things you have done. For example, a placement firm might search key terms like *VP, Product Development, BA, P&L management, engineering, six sigma,* or any other key words they consider qualifications for their open position. You want to show up in that search, so list as many key terms in your bio as possible. You have to know what kind of job you are looking for and then think about the kinds of key words a placement service might use when searching for people to fill that job. Joe Saad, president and founder of Diag Partners, said, "LinkedIn is the single most important tool in our company bar none. Nothing compares to it." If you want to get offers from recruiting firms like Diag make sure your personal email is somewhere on your LinkedIn page.

- EDUCATION | List all the schools you have attended and all degrees or certificates you have completed. For those of you who have education outside of college, list the coursework you have done. Companies want to see continued education throughout a career. This shows them you are a lifelong learner and always advancing. My Harvard professor said that an education today has a shelf life of three years. If you have not continually kept up with industry trends, technology, additional education, etc., then you are out of date and behind your peers. Continue to learn, and stay plugged into your industry. It has been said that in this new economy you don't earn a living, you *learn* a living. Being a continual learner is critical to getting employment and keeping it.

- RECOMMENDATIONS | Get as many recommendations as possible from leaders and people of influence. Yes, it is wonderful that your mom wrote something nice about you, but that is expected. Get your professors to endorse your work. Did you do something for your school or work on a special project where you rubbed shoulders with senior leaders? See if you can get the dean or president of the school to write a letter of recommendation. This carries a lot of weight. Many people will specifically sign up for positions and volunteer for work so they can get noticed by these types of leaders and hopefully get a recommendation from them in the future.

- GROUPS, CLUBS, AFFILIATIONS | LinkedIn has a great service allowing groups to create their own pages. Sign up to be a part of key groups that are within your area of expertise or interest. There are groups for sales, marketing, industry trades, etc. Belonging to these groups and participating in their functions not only keeps you in the loop regarding developments in your area of expertise, but it also allows you to network and stay posted on new job developments. Many placement firms searching for a specific type of person will start searching the members of key groups.

- UPDATE | Don't just create an account and let it lie there dormant. You need to check it daily. Who is viewing your account?

IF LINKEDIN IS YOUR ONLINE RESUME, FACEBOOK IS YOUR ONLINE BACKGROUND CHECK.

How many hits do you get? You can tell if placement firms are reviewing your page. Contact them and start a dialogue. Most important, start communicating on your account. Let people know you are searching for your next opportunity. Post here just like you would on Facebook, but remember the context. This is a business account and your online resume, so everything should relate in some way to that. This is not the place to post pictures of your dog balancing milk-bones on her head.

If LinkedIn is your online resume, Facebook is your online background check. Imagine your employer coming over and sitting in your home and saying they just wanted to watch you for a few days to get to know the "real you." That is how they are viewing Facebook—it is the first step to a background check. Girls-gone-wild videos, Insane Clown Posse photos, and radical political views might be okay with your friends but will cause a prospective employer to think twice about setting up an interview and offering you a job. Our goal is to remove all barriers to the interview and job offer. Our goal is for them to *want* you to be a part of their team. Imagine if you had two or three firms all recruiting you at the same time. Wouldn't you love that? Now you are in a position of power, can ask for certain things, and can take the best offer you are presented.

Much like LinkedIn, Facebook not only allows but encourages you to post as much background information on yourself as you are comfortable with. Here are the pages you need to review.

• ABOUT | Fill this out with your background information, current job, past jobs, education, personal websites or blogs, and contact information. More information here is better. Again, an account that is not complete raises questions. They might think you are hiding something or that you are not very tech savvy and don't know how to use or leverage social media in business. You want them to see you as open and transparent, and many companies today want their staff members to be well-versed in social media. If you can demonstrate competence in this area you will already be setting yourself apart from other candidates.

• PHOTOS | You want some great pictures here. Show off your vacations, work trips, birthday parties, holidays, and have fun! Just don't have photos of you doing anything that is unprofessional. Your online profile should not be devoted to the craziness of your youth or, worse yet, showing you have not grown up and still participate in sorority-style living. All firms have the unwritten rule, "Morons need not apply."

• LIKES | You can tell a lot about a person by what they "like." Fill out your music and film preferences and show a good variety of films you enjoy. Your book list is a great place to show your reading and continued education. As the old saying goes, "All leaders are readers." Don't lie and list books you have not read. You will get asked questions about these items and you want to speak intelligently about the topics. If you are not reading, I highly encourage you to do so. My recommended reading list for young professionals can be found at www.RobertDickie.com.

• BRANDS | This may sound trite, but the brands you like and follow say a lot about your taste and background. Marketers can see what products and brands you "like" and have a good idea what other products and services you are likely to buy. Employers can learn a lot from this as well. Make sure the brands and products you like are congruent with the image you want portrayed in the public eye.

• CONTENT! | This is, if you couldn't tell already, the most important aspect of your Facebook profile. Yes, Facebook is a mechanism of communicating with your friends and family, but your content—posts, likes, and public conversations—say a lot about you. Don't think this is private. Make sure everything you post is in alignment with how you want to be portrayed publically. We all have seen public reputations and careers wrecked as a result of a bad photo gone viral or one wrong comment. If your comments can be taken the wrong way, can be taken out of context, or are insensitive on any number of hot-button public issues, you are opening yourself up for trouble. When in doubt, don't shout it out—hit delete!

These services can be utilized for many different things. Headhunters and placement services will see LinkedIn as your online resume, Facebook as an online background check, and Twitter as personality assessment. Tweets on Twitter tend to be raw, unpolished, and many times highly emotional thoughts about life events, sports, or poor customer service. They can also be a short, bland, and monotonous quips about breakfast, your workout, or a disappointing day. These 140-character mini-blogs contain a wealth of information about you, your personality, your passions, and what makes you tick, sets you off, excites you, and upsets you. A trained psychologist can infer a great deal about you by reviewing your Twitter account. The more senior the position you are applying for is, the more these types of things are analyzed.

I was a personal reference for a highly trained and seasoned executive who was the president of a billion-dollar division of a major multinational corporation. He was in the running with three other candidates to be the CEO of a multi-billion-dollar global company. As a reference, I was given a lengthy assessment to fill out on this leader and then asked many questions about his temperament, abilities, and personality, how he handles stress, how he handles success, and every possible facet of his personal life. Much was riding on this publically traded company picking the right leader as its next CEO, and personality mattered a great deal. The lengths they went to while conducting background checks were amazing. Do you think they were looking at his social media sites and analyzing everything he was writing? You bet they were. Even if you are applying for a job at Starbucks, these items are important, and the wrong things on these sites can and will hurt your chances of getting employed. If you want to progress in your career, take great care of all your social media sites and the image you are portraying. You are building a brand. The question is, will your brand be one that a major company wants to invest in? It is all up to you.

> **I RECOMMEND YOU MAKE SURE THAT ALL THE CONTENT ENHANCES YOUR BRAND OR AT LEAST DOES NOT DETRACT FROM IT.**

Finally, videos have recently become more and more prevalent on the Internet. Google has actually changed its algorithms to make videos more important in search. This starts getting into more advanced brand-building and management, but it is important to mention it here. If you do not have a personal channel on YouTube, don't feel the need to start one just to have content. You need to start this *only* if you have a purpose and passion you want to talk about. However, if you do have a presence on YouTube or other video sites, these videos will start to rank higher and higher when a search is done on your name. You want great content associated with your name.

I recommend you make sure that all the content enhances your brand or at least does not detract from it. If you have a passion project or something that is very important to you, start talking about it. Leverage your expertise and knowledge to become seen as an expert on that particular subject. I have a friend who is an expert on gardening and building a life "off the grid." I have another who is focused on a specific type of investing. Whatever it is, find your niche and provide insightful and compelling research and commentary on that subject. Ideally, this will be something that is in alignment with the area you are looking to be employed in. If you have a degree in education and are applying for teaching positions, you should develop videos on YouTube showing you in action as you teach students and talk about your concepts for education.

If these videos provide great instruction for people needing help on a particular subject and do it in a unique groundbreaking way, this would help you. Khan Academy started this way and eventually received over $16.5 million in investments from the Bill and Melinda Gates Foundation, Google, and others.[1] Showing competence on your subject matter only further validates your resume and shows your talents in a real way, helping you make a great impression. These are free tools—use them to your advantage.

In closing, these are just the beginning steps on how to build and leverage your online social media presence as you look to land your next job. There are many more steps in the process that will come later. Never assume that once you get your job you are finished. The work is just starting. You need to continue to build your online presence and expertise in these areas. This is where many new opportunities will arise. Maybe a big promotion will come because of what people see. Many times other companies will try to hire away great talent that they want in their company or organization. It never hurts to have offers coming in! It feels great to be in a position where you have multiple offers from companies and can turn them down if they are not right for you. Sooner or later, a job will probably come around that you are very interested in, and you will be ready to take the leap. When that job is offered, it means people have found you and researched you via your online profile and social media—and it means they liked what they saw.

LEAPING BY EXAMPLE

LEVERAGING SOCIAL MEDIA: Kari Jobe, *musician and singer,*
Grammy-nominated artist

"Social media for me has been helpful, but it is also a great responsibility. So many people are listening to me, and I don't want to make a mistake. I need to be honest, uplifting, and encouraging." With over 1.5 million Facebook fans and 509,000 Twitter followers, Kari takes social media very seriously. Although it is a great way to connect with her fans, she is quick to note, "Social media is not going to make or break you. It is just a tool. I am really careful to make sure that my fans know it is me. I can tell when something is not real. Because of that I don't let others control my social media. People want to connect with me, and then they start to trust me. This is a way for me to let them into my life. It isn't a sales gimmick for me. There is a great deal of trust that I have built, but it requires a lot of time. The key is to be personal, vulnerable, and to be real. Just be present."

Kari says with a laugh, "I'm dorky! They love it. They love the silly stuff that happens to me. They retweet when I am having a bad day . . . and people send me encouraging messages. I want to be an encouragement back to them. It is all about meeting them where they are. The next generation loves community. This is the best way to build it with them."

At 33 years old, Kari's soft-spoken and humble voice is a refreshing contrast to the more self-centered promotion that many with her accolades generally use to accelerate their rising stardom. Her first album in 2009 rose to #67 on the Billboard and #1 on iTunes Christian music chart, which later resulted in a Grammy nomination and three Dove Award nominations (two of which she won). Through all this she has remained grounded, seeking to stay true to her calling of ministry to others. "If I am going through a diffi-cult time, I want to use that to help others. I want to share my stories and be an encouragement to others."

Her advice to those who are looking to use their social media to make a difference in the world while also differen-tiating themselves from the crowd: "I have found that those who know their true identity have a great social media pres-ence. Those who don't know their identity really struggle. Don't exploit yourself trying to get followed. Don't try to find your identity through social media. How many followers you have or how many "likes" you receive means nothing. Know who you are, and do what you are called to do. Be a person of influence, not a person who is influenced. Put yourself in a place where you are giving life to others."

Kari's parting words were, "God has opened this door for me. It is a ministry before anything else. The best advice I could give anyone in life is to create a well-worn path between you and God so you can get to Him quickly. Knowing God's voice has been how I have gotten through. I follow the peace of God, and that has guided my life. God will take you on a journey that you could never take yourself on." It is easy to see that Kari's success in music, her career, and connecting with those she feels called to serve has been because she is focused on serving rather than self-promoting. That is something to remember as you embark on your journey to take the leap!

STICKING THE LANDING

- Update all your social media accounts to ensure they represent you and your brand properly.

- Delete anything that would detract from your goals.

- Monitor your LinkedIn account regularly. As your online resume, this should be an ever-changing profile with updates and additions. Always check to see who is viewing your profile. This might clue you in on who is interested.

If you need help setting up your social media, marketing, or branding strategy for your company I recommend LimeBiscuit.com. They are an excellent agency I have worked with. Contact them at info@limebiscuit.com.

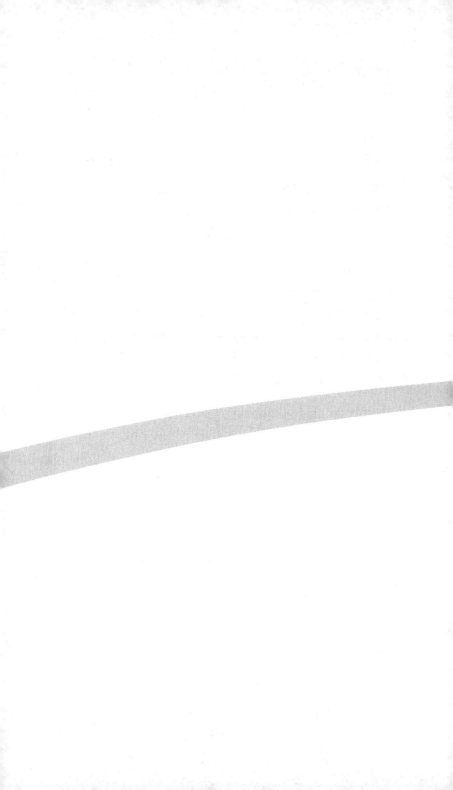

CHAPTER 8

EXPAND YOUR NETWORK

"Networking is an essential part of building wealth."
—ARMSTRONG WILLIAMS

"Your network is the most valuable asset you have when you are searching for a new job!" This is the most common statement I get from industry insiders at placement firms all around the country. When pressed further, many will say it is as important as your education. In my conversation with Katie King at Grant Thornton, she said, "You must be connected. It is a game-changer. You have to be on LinkedIn, but just because you are on social media does not mean you are connected. The younger generations are connected and social on their networks but are many times confused how to network in person." Winning in the game of networking, just like every other aspect of preparing to take the leap, will require focused attention and a plan. A network will only be as valuable as the time invested to build and maintain it and, like a garden, it requires constant maintenance if you expect to be able to harvest it one day.

This year I spoke with multiple CEOs of large head-hunting and employment firms from around the country trying to understand their industry and how people can improve their chances of finding a new job. Here are three interesting facts I learned:

- Most jobs are not advertised. They are filled internally and by word of mouth. The *Wall Street Journal* even noted that 80 percent of jobs are not publically advertised.[1]

- Placement firms are looking for candidates online, and the number-one place they look is LinkedIn. Joe Saad, the CEO and founder of Diag Partners, says 75 percent of their online placements are found here and then they move down the list with other resources as they seek out qualified candidates for positions they are trying to fill for their clients.

- A person's online profile matters. Once a person becomes a serious candidate for a position, search firms will look at all their social media outlets to get a "total" picture of the person they are recruiting before they contact them with an offer. One executive said, "Like it or not, everyone is quickly judged by their online presence. If there is something that is questionable, we move on to the next candidate, and they will never get called."

Those who are without work or looking for their next opportunity must understand it is critical that their network of friends, family, former business associates, and all social media contacts know that they are on the market. I am convinced that success in this new economy favors those who understand networking and leverage all assets available to them to their fullest potential.

If you are not investing in building your network, I highly encourage you to start today. This is one of the greatest assets that you can develop over your career that can be leveraged for many things. The time and energy you will put into your network daily will pay off when you need it most.

As valuable as your network is, many people are totally confused how to leverage it. When people hear the word *networking*, many have a knee-jerk reaction conjuring up negative images from the past. Networking can sound cold and impersonal, and for those of us who have experienced the self-absorbed networker who was only in it for their benefit, it is easy to understand why someone might say they don't want to do that. However, when we understand what networking really is and we have a paradigm shift, some might say networking is one of the most rewarding activities of business.

> **AS YOU BUILD RELATIONSHIPS WITH PEOPLE, ALWAYS BE LOOKING FOR WAYS TO PROVIDE VALUE TO THEM.**

Networking is simply connecting with people and building meaningful relationships. It is all about building trust. The next part is the most important: as you build relationships with people, always be looking for ways to provide value to them. A secret is to seek first to give, not receive, in this relationship. A mark of a master networker is one who is always looking to provide value to their relationships. Master networkers never view networking as an activity for personal gain. The ones who do are easy to spot. True networkers are genuine people who build friendships and relationships everywhere they go. They offer advice and assistance to everyone they meet. They use their network of friends and acquaintances to connect people, if it will bring value to both parties. Being kind and helping others is rewarding and it brings the purest joy in life to those who do it regularly. When we see it in this light, it is not as intimidating. Master networkers see networking as a way to help others. Rick Kuhlman, the founding director of the Knoxville Fellows Program, mentors a new group of young leaders each year in Knoxville. When asked how he views networking and how he teaches it in the Fellows program, he said, "Bob, I teach them that it is all about earning the right to sit at the table. When you build relationships with other leaders and become trusted, you earn the right to sit at the table where decisions are being made. The reason you want to sit at the table is because at that point you can be the most effective in helping others. You now are in a position to connect other people and help them through your influence and position. Networking is all about helping other people." In my mind, Rick's explanation summed it up perfectly. You'll hear from him more at the end of this chapter.

Networking makes us smarter people with broader world experiences and perspectives. I intentionally try to build relationships with people from around the globe so I can learn from them and see the world through their eyes. One of the most rewarding times of the year is when I attend the Harvard Business School YPO Presidents' Program. With over 180 CEOs and presidents from every continent, I always learn a great deal from the in-depth discussion on global issues and I walk away with new friends. This educational experience cannot be duplicated by reading a newspaper or watching the news. Networking will provide you with your best educational experiences.

With the right focus, we can build a network that helps us better understand the world and different perspectives. We will learn about other industries and changes in the economy and how they might impact us. Most importantly, we are in a position to help others make a difference in the world. I realize there may be some that still think they will never make good networkers. If that is you, remove the word *networker* from your vocabulary and in its place use *relationship-builder*. Many times the hang-up is with the word. Do you know of someone in your life who seems to be loved by everyone, have friends everywhere they go, and always seems to be trying to help people? They may not call themselves a *networker*, but they have mastered the skills to build and maintain relationships. This is not just for the gregarious, outgoing extroverts. Some of the best relationship-builders I have met are introverted and quiet-mannered people who are thoughtful and intentional in how they build relationships with people.

I try to spend a little time each week on maintaining the network of friends and relationships I have around the world. It is very rewarding. By staying in touch with those in my network, I feel more connected and knowledgeable about global events by getting accounts of global news from people experiencing it firsthand. I am always looking for ways to help and provide value to my friends, and in turn sometimes they have been able to help me. When we start with the right mindset and focus, we see networking is very different from how others may perceive it. If you start with the end objective, "To make the world a better place," you will be blessed in the process.

When building and developing your network, remember these four words: *secure, expand, leverage,* and *give.*

SECURE

First, we need to secure our base. We don't start building our network of relationships by merely going to conferences, collecting business cards from attendees, and filing them away. Likewise, going on to LinkedIn and connecting with random people is less than useful. We need to take stock of our current relationships. Building a network starts with those closest to you. View your network with close, concentric circles radiating outward. Your strongest relationships are closest to the center and thus have the greatest value. The relationships you have with people you can call at 2:00 a.m. who will drop everything to help you are the most valuable and are at the center of your circle.

These relationships are generally family and a few close friends who you can trust with your life. It can take a lifetime to build this type of relationship. If you have a handful of people like that in your life, you are a blessed individual.

As you take stock of the relationships in your life, it is important to start drawing connections between people, industries, passions, current projects, family situations, etc. The more you understand

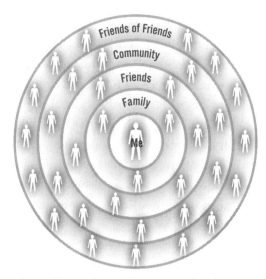

about your key relationships, the more value you will be able to provide them. A few years ago I was working with a national non-profit, and I learned the board was going through a rotation and they were looking for new leaders to add to the team. I knew the CEO and members of the board and told them about a close friend of mine who was a prominent businessman and very aligned with the mission of this organization. I knew it would be a win-win for both parties. I helped facilitate the meeting, and shortly thereafter that businessman became a member of the board. He has helped them revamp the organization and brought great value to this national nonprofit. He has enjoyed being able to serve in a capacity on a project he has been passionate about most of his adult life. By knowing the needs of the board and understanding the passions of my friend, I was able to bring value to both of these relationships. This is why deeply understanding your relationships and keeping your eyes and ears open is important. As a side note, not long after this meeting my friend returned the favor by recommending me for a very important project with another prominent organization in the United States. Always look to serve and help others, and it will come back to you.

Another part of securing our relationships is to make sure we are taking the time
to maintain contact with them. "Out of
sight, out of mind" is a saying we all have
heard, and with our busy lifestyles it is easy
to let months go by without communicating with key relationships in our lives. This
is something that cannot happen. Make it a
point to invest time every week sending out
a few emails or messaging a couple of contacts on LinkedIn or Facebook just to say

**MAKE IT A POINT
TO INVEST TIME EACH
DAY SENDING OUT
A FEW EMAILS OR
MESSAGING A COUPLE
OF CONTACTS ON
LINKEDIN OR
FACEBOOK JUST
TO SAY HELLO.**

hello. I try to routinely send a message to contacts saying, "Hey, I
was just thinking about you today. I trust things are going well. How
is the family? I just wanted to stay in touch. Let me know if there is
anything I can help you with." Many times as I am reading, I come
across an article that is relevant to someone and I will quickly send
it to them saying, "I thought you might enjoy this article. I know
this is in your industry and you were talking about this the last time
we spoke. All the best." Just today I received a lengthy PowerPoint
presentation with amazing industry data that I knew would be relevant to a classmate of mine at Harvard. He sits on the board of a
major private equity firm with a large investment in a publically
traded company that is experiencing some challenges. I sent him
the PowerPoint and said, "I received this today and I thought it
would be helpful to you. Let me know if I can help you with anything. Looking forward to seeing you in January." Shortly thereafter
I received an email back saying, "Bob, this was beyond informative!
Please keep any further related material coming. I hope you and
I can meet up soon." These are just little ways in which you can
provide value to your relationships daily. Your network is useful,
powerful, and valuable, but only as much as you provide value to
others first. Commit at least a few minutes each day to providing
value to your relationships. These are the most important people in

your life, and no matter what happens they will always be there for you. Regardless of what you do in life, never neglect these relationships. Over time your base (your most valuable relationships) in the inner circle will grow.

EXPAND

Secondly, we need to expand our network of relationships. It is easy for us to get complacent and stay in our comfort zone. We all have our routines in life and over time our relationships will consist of the same people from our places of work, neighborhoods where we live, schools we attended, our place of worship, and maybe a local club we joined. If we don't venture outside those standard spheres, our network will be limited. This is where joining global organizations and nonprofits, attending industry conferences, and traveling will open doors and help expand our relationships. The more we are able to expand our network of relationships outside our normal daily paths, the more valuable it will become.

Recently I have come in contact with multiple people who for the vast majority of their career spent no time networking and building relationships within their industry. Having known one in particular for many years, the common theme was, "I don't have time to play politics and get involved in organizations and committees and be a part of my industry. I am happy here in my small corner of the world minding my own business." The problem however was this leader late in life was faced with some challenges where having an industry network to draw on to help him with his problems was critical and he had no one to call. He had "played it safe" by not venturing out to expand his network and now he was all alone. Take the time to build relationships, and not just in your small corner of the world or in your industry, but expand your relationships and reach into as many related areas as possible. It will help you to be interconnected and have a wide range of relationships across many industries.

To build a larger network, I highly encourage you to look at regional, national, and even global organizations. Locally you may want to join Toastmasters or the chamber of commerce to start meeting business leaders in your area. Many churches and non-profits have regional and national organizations to associate with and are always looking for volunteers. Since your time is limited, link up your passions with the organizations you will serve on. For those looking for global business organizations, I highly recommend Young Presidents' Organization (YPO), Entrepreneurs Organization, Giant Leadership Core, and C12. I worked with the Autism Society in Washington, D.C. and other nonprofits around the United States and it has been some of the most rewarding work of my life through which I met people that have become lifelong friends.

Attending leadership conferences that bring in people from many different industries and walks of life is also a great way to grow your network. Some of my favorite conferences are the GiANT Impact Leadercast, The Global Leadership Summit, Christian Economic Forum, TED Talks, South by Southwest, and Catalyst. If you have never attended a conference like these, I highly encourage you to attend one and you will understand the benefits. These are some of the best networking events I have attended, and I walk away each year with new friends and contacts from around the globe.

LEVERAGE

Thirdly, learn to leverage free tools and resources to grow and maintain your network. I only have the ability to invest in building a few really deep relationships in my life at any one time, so I have to be strategic where I invest that energy yet still have time to keep up with contacts from around the globe. I can't have coffee twice a week and talk about my start-up project with my friend in Dubai like I can with my close friends in Knoxville. However, I can stay in touch and invest in that relationship by communicating via Google Hangout once a month. I use various forms of communication to stay in touch with hundreds of other friends around the world. Luckily, we live in an age where we can leverage technology to stay in touch. My favorites are LinkedIn, Facebook, Twitter, Instagram, Google+, and Google Hangout. You can use each one to offer a unique view into your life and to communicate with your friends. The more you communicate and share your life with others, the closer you draw them to the center of your relationship circle. They become part of your life and sometimes part of your extended family.

One of my favorite services is Newsle.com You can sign up and link your contacts list on Facebook and LinkedIn with the service. Anytime one of your contacts is in the news (local newspaper, national paper, magazine, press release, etc.), you will get an email with a link to the piece. I routinely get emails about a friend or business contact who is in the news for landing a big deal, selling a company, retiring, or having a product launch, and I will use that as

THE MORE GENEROUS YOU ARE, THE MORE VALUABLE YOUR NETWORK BECOMES.

an opportunity to send them an email. It might simply be "Lisa, I see it is official! Congrats on the retirement and best of luck in the next chapter in life. I look forward to seeing what you do next. All the best, Bob." This is just an easy way to keep in touch with people when they have something important going on in their life.

Here is one secret I will share. It is almost expected in the United States that your closest relationships will receive a "holiday card" around Christmas or New Year's. This is a perfect time to stay in touch with your network of friends, family, and business relationships. Over the years, my wife and I have developed a list of hundreds of friends from the military, various businesses, church, and locations where we have lived around the country. We feel it is important to reach out to everyone at Christmas and give them a brief update. My wife, Brandi, refers to herself as the "mama-razzi," due to the copious number of pictures she takes of our family, so she designs a special card each Christmas that tells a story of the year in pictures. We send this out to hundreds of friends, family, and key business relationships, and this is an important touch point for us each year. Another secret is to send out your card at a random time during the year. With everyone getting hundreds of cards at Christmas, it is easy to get lost in the noise. We have sent a "Happy Thanksgiving" card in November to be the first in the mail and we have sent a "Happy New Year" card a week into January so that we know people get it.

GIVE

Finally, in everything you do with building relationships, think about connecting people and providing value to them. Some people will look to build a network to extract value from it, and these people will not be successful. If you follow the rule to "Give before you ask," you will build a valuable network of people who will come to your aid when you need it most. Always be monitoring your network of friends and relationships and looking for ways to help them. It may be with advice, introductions to key relationships that can help with a project, sending them a business deal you know about, or a whole host of other possibilities.

There is one key rule in networking: the more generous you are, the more valuable your network becomes. I have found there is no such thing as a self-made man or woman. Even the most successful men and women in the world once had help from mentors, advisors, and people who helped open doors and gave them an opportunity. We all need help at various points of our lives. I am forever in debt to the many who have filled this role in my life. Those people who helped me in times of my greatest need can call me at any time of the day, and no matter what I am doing I will drop everything to come to their aid. I know there are people who will do the same for me. Over time as you look to serve others and help people within your network, you will build up enormous social equity. The next time you are in a career transition, looking for work, needing assistance on a project, or having a life issue and need help, you will be surprised at how many people will be excited to help the person who once helped them.

Building relationships is one of the most rewarding things you can do in life. It just so happens to be good for your career as well.

LEAPING BY EXAMPLE

EXPAND YOUR NETWORK: Colonel Rick Kuhlman, *(Ret.) Knoxville Fellows, director*

Each year, a new class of 16 dynamic young leaders enters the Knoxville Fellows program under the watchful eye and mentorship of Rick Kuhlman, the founding director of the program. The retired United States Air Force colonel leads with a soft voice and caring heart, and his years of work in Knoxville have made him one of the most networked men in town. He says he believes most people are only two phone calls away from any person they want to speak with. His networking ability has helped build the Knoxville Fellows program into one of the premier national fellowships, and his mentorship of the young men and women that graduate each year has helped them all transition into great careers.

Rick says that networking is one of the most important components of the program. "A network is critical in this job market. We strategically work to get in front of leaders, not asking for anything like a job, but seeking advice and providing help when needed. The key to building your network is to understand it is about trust and relationships." Rick teaches each class to get outside of their comfort zone and to go to functions where they can engage with local leaders on a regular basis. "This is a skill you have to develop. It just takes practice but it really pays off," said Rick. "You have to earn the right to get a callback. That comes by building relationships with people and having them trust you. When you need it most, those friendships will be able to help you." Building your network will take time and patience, but if you practice daily, look for ways to get outside your comfort zone, and always first look to provide value to others and help them with their projects and needs, you will quickly build a powerful network.

STICKING THE LANDING

- Make a list of the people you could call at two in the morning if you had an emergency. Who do you have relationships with that would drop everything to help you in a time of crisis?

- Make a list of people you would call to help you if you lost your job tomorrow. This list needs to be people of influence, business leaders, people who do hiring for companies, contacts at placement firms, etc. More importantly, if you have a dream to work in a specific industry or company, you should start developing relationships inside those organizations today.

- Your goal is to grow both of these lists over time. If you have not been in contact with a person on these lists within the last 90 days, put a plan in place to start staying in touch with them on a regular basis. If you have not provided value in their lives in the last year, be looking for ways to help them and provide value. You want to build up a reserve of goodwill so that if you ever call them and need their help they will be excited to be able to return the favor.

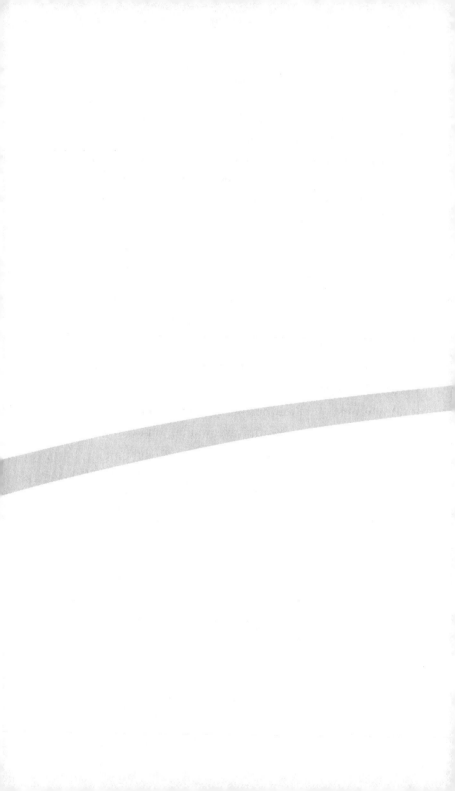

CHAPTER 9

JOIN
THE
TEAM

"Perseverance is the hard work you do after you get tired of doing the hard work you have already done." —NEWT GINGRICH

The stress of unemployment can slowly build a mental purgatory of negative thoughts that alter your mood, behavior, and outlook. Without a support team and a positive attitude, I have seen people slowly self-destruct while battling long-term unemployment. The stress during this time can be almost insurmountable. In our society, people often have their self-worth tied up in their job or title and their ability to earn an income, provide for their family, and be self-reliant. We know that this is wrong and that our identity and value should not be based in our work, but unless you have gone through the situation where one day you wake up and it is all gone, you won't understand how it impacts your soul. This has been a national epidemic in the past five years—mid-career professionals being displaced and suffering from depression that comes with losing a job, security, a paycheck, and everything that comes with a career that once seemed to provide identity. One of the best books

I have read on changing your mindset related to a job and career is *The True Measure of a Man* by Richard Simmons.

For those currently unemployed, I want to help you change your perspective on the situation. It is important to have a positive outlook and act from a position of strength, hope, and courage. We have discussed the importance of an internal locus of control. Another secret about taking action is that it reduces stress, because we feel a little more in control when we work to actively change our situation. Another little secret . . . no one will want you employed more than you. Our effort and energy in landing the next role determines our success. We need to be relentless, driven, taking intentional action toward our goal, and kicking down any obstacles that are in our way. I have witnessed those who have this level of determination. They are able to accomplish anything they set their minds to.

IN THE NEW ECONOMY, A RESUME IS THE END OF THE PROCESS, NOT THE START.

For those who are unemployed and looking to secure a position within a new company, one of the best ways to do this is to volunteer or intern at that company. I call this "joining the team." The least effective way to secure the job of your dreams is to spam multiple organizations with your resume and sit back and wait to hear from them or passively post your resume on Monster.com or TheLadders.com. As the number of unemployed rise, HR departments are flooded with aspiring applicants. These "gatekeepers" are tough to circumvent. From my years of experience, most hires—especially at the senior levels within an organization—are "sponsored" by a senior leader who helps the candidate get them past the gatekeeper.

In fact, another paradigm shift needs to occur. In the past, the resume was the start of the hiring process. People would work on it and maybe even hire a consultant to help them craft it just right. Then this finely tuned piece of paper that tried to encapsulate the essence of a person, their value to the world, and bullet points of achievements was whisked off to all sorts of businesses in hopes it would catch someone's eye and elicit an interview. Employers and employees alike placed utmost importance on it, to the point where it was overdone. In the new economy, a resume is the end of the process, not the start. If you do decide to go through the gatekeepers, through the online job-posting sites with the millions of others, that piece of paper has to be better than everyone else's because that is how you will be judged, even before your interview. However, I encourage you to take a better route. Sidestep the traditional method, heading directly to the decision-maker. When you do this, your resume comes into play at the end of the process, and many times you will never even be asked for it!

In the new world, relationships matter most of all, and your results and reputation go before you. That is the best resume you can work on. I know countless people who have been offered jobs and been hired who never had to produce a resume or even had their references called. Why? They were working with senior decision-makers in the organization, and their work, reputation, and brand went before them and opened the door. If you had to choose, which route would you take?

Earlier we discussed networking and building key relationships in advance before you need them. This is when all that work pays dividends. If you get a solid recommendation from a senior leader of the organization, you are set. When a member of the senior leadership team walks into the Human Resources department and says, "I want to hire Amy as a member of my team," rest assured Amy will be a member of the team. HR, like everyone else, wants to keep the boss happy. In many respects, HR and the official hiring process is the "backup" hiring process if the leaders are not able to leverage their own network to find the right candidate. Katie King said, "Leaders want to work with people they know and trust. Your personality is key. Like it or not, people hire people they like and can get along with and enjoy being around."

Many times leaders go to their own network and industry circles first when a position comes open. Only if the leader or the team members cannot find a great candidate within their network will they turn to Human Resources or a recruiter to bring them candidates to consider. Your goal should be to get in that network, get noticed by senior leadership, and have them "sponsor" you so you don't have to rely on the normal channels. To do this . . . join the team!

As you will see, getting hired is a multifaceted approach where you can be pursuing multiple avenues at once. In fact, it is critical you are working three strategies in unison. Remember to announce, network, and join.

ANNOUNCE

To begin with, you need to announce to the right people that you are on the market and looking. If possible, you want to start leveraging key contacts within your network before you make your transition. This is a very sensitive time. You need counsel and guidance on what to do for your next step, but you don't want blowback within your own organization. If word gets back to your coworkers or management that you are looking to transition, some leaders could take action to replace you before you are ready to go. You need to be very careful who you bring into your confidence and discuss your plans with. When I was in the military, officers were very cautious never to tell their chain of command if they were thinking of "getting out" well in advance of their planned separation date because they would be treated as a part-timer and potentially get the least desirable assignments while others would get more personal attention and get groomed for future promotions. My very first commander, LTC Gary Gibbs, gave a group of young second lieutenants great advice when he said, "Until you put in your separation paperwork, everyone in the Air Force should think you are making this a career and you plan on being in for 30 years. If they think otherwise, you are guaranteed to be treated differently." I never forgot that advice, and it holds true in the civilian world as well. You want to be seen as a "company man" until you aren't. With that said, I am not saying to be dishonest or make a transition that puts your organization in harm's way or hurts your coworkers. I have just never seen a situation where giving an employer a heads-up that you are thinking of making a career move worked out well for the employee. Although there are times when a quick departure is warranted, the vast majority of the time, giving a few weeks' notice, based on your position, is the norm and perfectly acceptable.

KNOWING THE HIRING PROCESS IS IMPORTANT; KNOWING THE PEOPLE IS CRITICAL.

If you are unemployed, the situation is much easier. You should issue an "all points bulletin" on every social network you are on and make sure everyone knows you are available and looking for your next opportunity. When you are in "job-search mode," you don't want any of your relationships thinking you are still employed and not interested in opportunities. Get the word out that you are readily available!

NETWORK

If you have zeroed in on a company you really want to work for in your local area, you need to take specific action by networking with key people in that company. Start by working with the company's HR department to see what jobs are currently available. Learn about the hiring procedures and get to know the entry level managers in charge of this process. What type of paperwork is required to be filled out? How does the entire process work? Who are the key leaders that make these decisions? Who are the department managers, division leaders, and senior leaders in the organization that you would be working for? This is just for intel-gathering. Your game plan is not to get hired through HR but to get sponsored by a senior leader within the company. The more information you know about the company, their processes, and the system they use to hire people for internal positions, the better prepared you can be. This will drastically increase your chances for gaining employment. Knowing the hiring process is important; knowing the people is critical.

JOIN

Finally, you need to join the team. Once you have notified key members in your network of your availability and you have networked with the HR departments at the top companies on your list, the next step is "getting inside." Don't stand on the outside waiting for a phone call. If it is your dream to work for a particular organization, stack the deck in your favor and find a way to join the team, even if you are not yet hired.

There are multiple ways to accomplish this. Most importantly, do you know anyone inside the company who can be an advocate for you and introduce you to the key people in the HR department and other leaders within the company? This person is able to help you navigate past the gatekeepers to the people of influence who are able to make decisions on your behalf. Having an internal advocate is one of the best methods to get inside a company. I have known people who dreamed of working for specific organizations and spent over a year developing friendships and relationships with members of an organization so they could have an internal advocate when the time was right to seek a job.

Internships are one of the best ways to get inside a company. Many companies use their internship programs as a way to get to know potential hires and to see how they perform on a daily basis. This is also a great way for the intern to truly know the culture and environment of a company prior to making a commitment to join the staff as an employee. If you are a solid team member adding value every day to the team and bringing energy, enthusiasm, and new ideas to the table, the leaders of the company will not want to see you go. You will have proven your value and they will be looking for ways to keep you on the team.

An example of this is Mike Townsend of Townsend Strategies in Knoxville, Tennessee. Mike started his consulting firm that specializes in working with tire dealerships, and through his years of experience he has developed systems that are proven to increase revenue, decrease cost, and help the organization run better. However, many small, locally owned tire dealerships see a "consultant" walking through their door and they don't know what to expect and are reluctant to hear a proposal. So Mike learned to make them a deal they can't refuse. He tells them about his results and the people he has worked with. He tells them what he can do for them and then says he will work for free on one condition . . . if they implement his strategy and he helps them save what he has projected, he will receive a percentage of the savings or profits. Mike has been blessed and is doing very well.

If you are unemployed and have not been able to secure your next gig, why not try the same thing? If you're having difficulty getting your foot in the door, make it easy for them. Craft a deal they can't refuse and then deliver big time! There is always a way to get in the door if you want it bad enough.

Three promising paths to get inside an organization and join their team in an official capacity are through internships, apprenticeships, and temporary employment (temp work).

INTERNSHIPS

Internships have generally been seen as a method for young people and college students to get work experience. If you are a mid-career professional in your 40s, 50s, or even 60s you may be thinking, *I am too old to be an intern . . . won't that look weird on my resume?* The answer is no. Call it whatever you want . . . internship, volunteering, consulting for free, it does not matter.

Many internships are low-pay, entry-level work, and some are even offered at no pay. Even though some of these assignments might be offered for grunt work, having worked with many interns personally I am convinced that if the intern approaches the assignment with the right attitude, along with energy and enthusiasm, and treats it like a full-time job, they will go far.

There are many national programs that structure full-time internships around education programs that provide yearlong assignments for prospective interns looking to get real-world experience, grow their resume, build their network, and gain additional education opportunities. I have worked extensively with the Fellows program in Knoxville, which is part of the Fellows Initiative, and I have been extremely impressed with the quality of the leadership, program curriculum, and interns that I have been fortunate to work with. I have worked with four interns and ended up hiring two to full-time positions in my organization. Both are young stars of high potential doing great work. The Fellows Initiative is a strategic way my organization is looking to hire talented and motivated professionals that we can groom into senior leaders for our organization. National programs like this offer great benefits and should be sought out in your local area.

APPRENTICESHIPS

Many Americans have forgotten about the tried and true apprenticeship programs of the past as a great way to pass education and skills down to the youth entering the workforce. An apprenticeship is generally a more advanced program than an internship, in which the apprentice gets paid to work in a specific area of skilled study along with a mentor providing a robust education program. Although this "Earn and Learn" method has been a common training for many blue-collar jobs and skilled trades, other industries like health care and technology are starting to use this method to train a younger workforce. Brad Neese, director of Apprenticeship Carolina, says, "College degrees and internships don't produce the same quality of worker as intensive, on-the-job apprenticeships."[1]

Although apprenticeships in America are not as prominent as they once were, they are still thriving worldwide. For example, the US has just 7 percent of the number of apprenticeships Great Britain has.[2] Policy makers see the apprenticeship route as a potential way to solve the growing unemployment problem with America's youth, which is now above 20 percent. Comparatively, Germany's youth unemployment is only 8 percent, due in large part to a well-developed and robust apprenticeship program for their young.[3] In an attempt to help jump-start this initiative, President Obama pledged $100 million in April of 2014 to new apprenticeship programs in key growth industries.[4] Sarah Ayres wrote a piece titled "5 Reasons Expanding Apprenticeships Will Benefit Millennials" for the Center for American Progress in which she says expanding apprenticeships in the US "would especially benefit Millennials, who are struggling with disproportionately high unemployment, low-wage jobs, rising college costs, and spiraling student debt. Apprenticeships can create promising new pathways for young workers to well-paying, middle class jobs."[5]

This method of "Earn and Learn" is proven, and with government and industry support it will be growing in the United States over the next decade. Look for local and state apprenticeships and search the Department of Labor for registered apprenticeships. This is a great option for workers wanting to be trained in a skill without taking on student-loan debt.

TEMPORARY EMPLOYMENT (TEMP WORK)

The temporary workforce worldwide has grown substantially since 2007 and experts see no slowing down. The US Department of Labor reported that 75 percent of the jobs created in 2013 were temporary.[6] With new policies impacting the US labor markets, many placement firm executives like Joe Saad foresee that the temporary workforce in the United States, which currently comprises 7.5 to 8.5 percent of the total workforce, will grow dramatically over the next 10 years. Many predict the US is moving quickly to a European system, where upwards of 19.5 percent of the workforce is part-time, and this number is only increasing.[7] In this low-growth market, it is commonly understood that companies see the temporary workforce as a way to protect profits. With temporary employees, you're saved the costs of providing full-time benefits. Due to certain laws, some career fields are harder to outsource than others. Some are much easier. Anything that is transactional and where staff can be interchanged quickly without hurting operations will be under threat of outsourcing. This would include transactional accounting like AR/AP and many functions in IT.

SOLVE PROBLEMS FOR THE ORGANIZATION, LIGHTEN YOUR BOSS'S WORKLOAD, RECOMMEND IMPROVEMENTS, AND OFFER TO TACKLE CHALLENGING PROJECTS THAT OTHERS HAVE AVOIDED.

Many temporary workers love the flexibility it offers and for some, temp work is the best work situation for them. For many who are looking for full-time employment, one common complaint about being part-time is the insecurity of not being a full-time employee. Not receiving the standard benefit package that full-time staff members receive is challenging, but the uncertainty of whether or not you will have work next week or next month is difficult to bear. This is another reason to reduce debt and bring your monthly overhead, or burn rate, down as much as possible. If you are in this situation, you can provide your own security and reduce stress by having a fully funded freedom fund, knowing that if you lose your job you will be able to pay your bills for an extended period of time while you look for your next job.

In this environment, landing a temporary job at a company could be a great way to get noticed and move into full-time employment. The key is to move quickly out of transactional work and into knowledge-based work with the company, where losing your experience and expertise would hurt the organization. Asking to take on more roles and responsibilities is also a way to expand your duties and add value to the organization. Solve problems for the organization, lighten your boss's workload, recommend improvements, and offer to tackle challenging projects that others have avoided. While you are excelling in your temporary assignment, work to impress and make friends with key influencers in the organization. Since many people are okay with being average and doing the minimum to get by, you may quickly rise to the top and be seen as a productive member of the team who is bringing value to the organization every day. It won't take long for your star to rise and for you to be brought on full-time.

As the temporary-job market continues to grow over the next 10 years, more and more of the jobs available will be through temp agencies and on a temporary basis. If your career field is one that is ripe to be disrupted by this change, it is critical to do two things. First, start working to get out of transactional work and into more knowledge-based work around the systems and internal workings of the organization. You will be hardwired into the DNA of the organization and difficult to replace with a temp worker. Second, develop the skill sets needed to be able to quickly be seen as a star player and move from a temp role into a full-time role. This might take some practice and exercise skills that you have not used before in your career. You need to know how to navigate politically within an organization, sidestepping issues and drama that can derail your efforts.

> **STRIVE TO IMPRESS THE STAFF EVERY DAY. MAKE IT YOUR MISSION TO WORK HARDER THAN EVERYONE ELSE.**

Early in my career, a friend advised that I read *Career Warfare: 10 Rules for Building a Successful Personal Brand and Fighting to Keep It* by David D'Alessandro. It is a great book with practical advice in navigating the many pitfalls of the corporate world.

In the end, take action daily, be intentional, and understand that getting inside is just the first step. Using the skills and discipline you have developed, strive to impress the staff every day. Make it your mission to work harder than everyone else. Radiate value, honesty, trustworthiness, and dependability, and do the work that no one else wants to do. Have an attitude of service before self, and in all you do set the standard of excellence. Bring a contagious attitude of enthusiasm and excitement and I promise you, that company will be looking for ways to hire you to be a long-term member of their team!

LEAPING BY EXAMPLE

JOIN THE TEAM: Chuck Bentley, *Crown, CEO*

From volunteer to CEO, Chuck Bentley's rise to become the leader of Crown is one to consider for those with the hope of joining a team in a full-time capacity. Ultimately, faith in the unseen and a passion for the cause fueled Chuck to stick with the course through all obstacles. His faithfulness has been rewarded with ever-increasing responsibility. Chuck was blessed by Crown's ministry many years ago and originally volunteered with a city team in Dallas to give back. During this time, through prayer and an encouragement from a friend who said he felt God was calling Chuck to full-time ministry, Chuck took the leap. He left an executive position in the business world to enter ministry—having to forgo the security of corporate life and raise his own support. "I had a wife and four children. My decision may have seemed risky to others, but it was the safest decision because I placed my life in God's hands. I had total peace about it, and God has been faithful," said Chuck. The journey continued to take twists and turns as Chuck rose to be the Area Director for Dallas, then the State Director for Texas, then the VP of Field Operations, and then the Senior VP for Global Impact before being chosen by Crown's late founder, Larry Burkett, to be the next CEO of the organization. Chuck remembers this road with fondness of all the joys and challenges that led him to shoulder the responsibility of the organization today. "It was humbling, leaving corporate America and taking what appeared to be a low-level job. But I got great joy serving in each position and trying to provide the best value I could to the organization. What may have looked like a blind leap was actually a step toward the greatest security I could experience, because I knew God was directing my path, not me." Chuck challenges those who are weighing the options of taking the leap to not consider the financial considerations of your choice. "The financial situation will change over time, for the better or the worse. You don't want to make a life decision based on finances. The best advice I can give is to discern what God is calling you to do and then do it fearlessly. Find out what you care about enough to give your life for, and then give your life to that cause. You will not have any regrets!"

STICKING THE LANDING

- If your goal is to secure employment in a certain company or organization, start to build relationships with members of the organization.

- See if you can volunteer and work on special internal or community service projects that are important to the organization. This will allow you to display your skills and build key relationships with members of the team.

- Find a local nonprofit and local business associations to volunteer with to build relationships with local leaders across multiple industries.

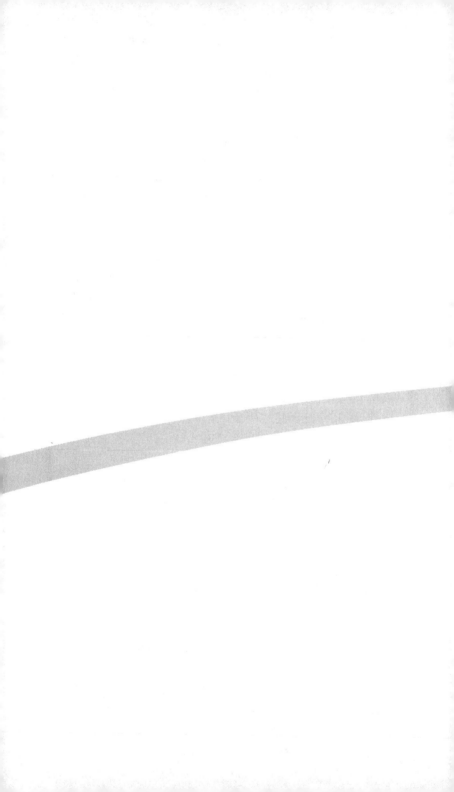

CHAPTER 10

PAY IT FORWARD

"Only a life lived for others is a life worth living."
—ALBERT EINSTEIN

Have you ever prayed for a miracle or asked yourself, *Do miracles really happen?* Some people might dismiss it as coincidence, luck, serendipity, or good karma, but I believe the miracles I have witnessed in my life are true answers of prayer. I have gone through tough times where I have literally been on my knees in prayer, asking for God's help, and through divine intervention my prayers have been answered.

Miracles do happen, and I believe God will often work through us to cause a miracle to happen in someone's life. We have to be listening and ready to act when we hear that voice in our head, and more often in our heart, telling us to take action to help someone.

This is why I feel this chapter is the most important. I have given tips on how to have success in this economy and the new part-time world we live in, and I hope they will help you navigate these challenging times. However, the act of serving others is the one I am most passionate about. It has the potential to change not only your life but the lives of those around you. **You** have the power to change

OUR STRESS FADES AWAY AS WE FOCUS ON OTHERS MORE.

the world one person at a time. You have the ability to help a miracle come to pass in someone's life and in the process increase their faith. If they pay it forward to someone else, it could start a ripple effect that stretches beyond your lifetime, impacting thousands. Think about it. What more important thing could you do? It all starts with helping one person.

Putting others first and truly caring about their well-being and success helps us to see the world differently and our problems or challenges become smaller. Our stress fades away as we focus on others more. It is no coincidence that the best sales people I know are genuinely concerned about their customers and their needs. Their own needs or personal sales goals, although important, come second. In the end, those with this type of mindset are the most successful people I have met. On the other hand, sales people I know and have worked with who struggle, never hit their numbers, and rotate from job to job—blaming the marketing or the product for their lack of success—are ones who are constantly focused on their own goals, numbers, and monthly paychecks with the customer's needs taking a backseat. I have seen this enough in my career to understand this is not just an anomaly within an industry. Those who put the needs of others before their own and give of themselves are the happiest and most successful people I know. Mark Twain is credited with saying, "Kindness is the language which the deaf can hear and that which the blind can see." Our ultimate success comes from caring enough to look past ourselves and our issues and helping others.

In the movie *The Pursuit of Happyness*, Will Smith plays the role of a man named Chris Gardner, who is a struggling salesman with every odd stacked against him. Although he is intelligent and hardworking, he simply cannot make ends meet and desperately needs help. He applies for a highly competitive unpaid internship in the hopes of one day becoming a stockbroker for a prestigious San Francisco firm. Although on paper many other candidates were more qualified, someone in the firm noticed something special about him during his interview and gave him a chance. That is all Chris needed. He seizes the opportunity and eventually became a star within the firm. He needed a miracle to happen in his life, and it came from someone willing to look past his appearance, his mistakes, and all the odds stacked against him and give him a chance.

A lesser known story but one that has been impacting people around the country is the story of Jon Katov, the CEO and Founder of OpenTable.org. Last year I had the opportunity to meet Jon, and his story and transformation deeply impacted me. Jon's journey of enlightenment and redemption are best told in his own words.

> At a young age, seeing the hurt in the world, including my own, caused me to judge God to be indifferent to human suffering. I told God that to make Him feel the sting of indifference, I would help no one. I would later learn to understand that God is not indifferent, but we as humans are, and our indifference to suffering is a ticket to greed.

> Almost thirty years later, my wife and I attended a church service at her suggestion. While the congregation sang and prayed, I taunted God. I called Him out to demonstrate a change in His character to see if He had moved from being an indifferent God to a God of good. Over the next several weeks, I continued to taunt while others praised.

> About a month later, I was driving home from work and saw many cars ahead of me stopped at a green light. I watched as the light continued to cycle from red to green without traffic moving. As frustration rose and drivers became impatient and honked their horns, I decided to see what was happening. I rolled down the

window, leaned out, and there she was. A confused and disoriented woman was stumbling around the middle of the intersection, unable to navigate her way to safety. I immediately judged her and became impatient. She was blocking my way and interrupting my daily plans . . . how dare her! Out of anger I pulled back my hand ready to lay on the horn in hopes that one more might solve the problem, but I suddenly heard a voice that I had not listened to for three decades. Strangely I was compelled to take a different course of action. So a man who told God he would live a life of indifference stepped onto the street and started walking toward the helpless lady in need. Then I started running toward her. As emotion came over me, I started crying. When I reached her with my outstretched arms, she fell into them, and I could sense her relief that someone finally cared enough to save her. I heard God saying, "Jon, I have been in this intersection yelling at My children to respond to the pain of this woman . . . and no one answered. I am wherever there is suffering, calling to this world to respond, but My children drive by their own brothers and sisters. If you want to find Me, just run to the tears instead of away from them."

WHILE HE KNEW HOW TO HAND AN ENERGY BAR OUT TO THE POOR, HIS CHURCH HAD NOT PREPARED HIM TO HAVE A DEEP AND MEANINGFUL CONVERSATION WITH THEM.

After helping this poor lady on her way, I went back to the church where I had previously taunted God. I spoke to the pastor and began a journey to try to empty myself of me and refill myself with God. I have learned this is a lifelong process. That moment in time radically changed my life and I am so thankful I am on this new journey.

This moment of spiritual enlightenment inspired Jon to get involved and help those in need, but his story does not stop there.

Seven years later, while with a group from his church that was helping pass out food at a homeless shelter, a man came through the line but did not want the energy bars, apples, or water. Instead, he wanted to speak to Jon's group and walked toward them. Jon recalls sensing an emergency as he watched the man walk closer. While he knew how to hand an energy bar out to the poor, his church had not prepared him to have a deep and meaningful conversation with them. Jon wondered how he would be caring while not making himself responsible for his needs. As the man stepped up to the group, he asked, "Can I worship at your church?"

"At that moment, I did not truly understand the meaning of what he was asking us. Now I know that his request to worship at our church meant, 'Please hear me! I am a child of God, and I need community and a relationship! I cannot restore myself.' When the poor we serve thank us for an energy bar, I wonder if they are thinking, *How do I use this to leave poverty?*"

The man's name was Phil and Jon's group fell in love with him. After Jon's group spent time searching for an organization who would help Phil and take responsibility for him, they finally faced the obvious: "We were the people we were looking for. We were there to heal and, though we did not know it, Phil was there to heal us."

Jon was a businessman at the time, so he recalls thinking of Phil as a broken Fortune 500 corporation in need of a new board of directors and a business plan. He told Phil the plan, and Phil agreed to be in partnership with them. John asked people at his church who had met Phil if they would join Phil's board of directors, develop a business plan with him for what his life could look like in a year, and use their occupational and life knowledge and personal connections to implement it. "We know now that a congregation has thousands of years of life and work experiences and personal networks that never have the opportunity to be invested in the poor because the church does not have a model built to invest the intellectual and social capital of its members." Jon told them they would meet with Phil as a board every week until Phil said he was satisfied.

For eight months, Phil's board of ten church members learned to meet Phil where he was, and he became financially sustainable. Relationship brought trust and trust brought good decision-making. They invested their vocational and life experiences and personal networks. Then, to their absolute surprise, Phil fired his board. He said he was tired of them being in his business and he could take it from there. And he did.

The goal of OpenTable.org is to move away from the old model of "transactional poverty-maintenance," where people are kept comfortable in poverty, to a highly relational model where mentors form strong relationships with those in poverty, helping them move out of poverty. This transformational approach is yielding great results around the country, and more leaders and mentors are needed to implement this program in more communities.

"After nine years, I continue in authentic relationship with Phil. I strive to be his safety net in case he ever falls toward poverty again, while he is my safety net if I ever fall from God's purpose for me," says Jon. This is exactly the intent of Open Table.

A man's life was changed, his paradigm radically altered, and he became a committed man with purpose to help others. Thus, OpenTable.org was born. An organization driven not to make people comfortable in poverty—poverty maintenance as Jon calls it—but to help end poverty one person at a time. It is time-consuming and requires each member to get deeply involved with personal mentorship and to walk alongside the poor as the restoration process takes place. This is the hard work that happens long after a donation check has been written. It is emulating the life that Christ lived—how He served and restored people. When people are committed to giving their lives, not just a donation, miracles can happen. It starts with us.

Every day there are deserving people who are praying for a miracle to happen in their lives, and many times that answered prayer will come from us hearing the voice in our head saying, "Give them a chance." I have been on the receiving end of those miracles, and they changed my life.

Now, there may be someone reading right now thinking, *I am that person in need! I need that miracle in my life today!* Maybe you are enduring struggles and have been unemployed and looking for work. Maybe you are on the verge of taking the leap and starting your own business, and you need help getting it started. No matter your situation, I encourage you today to step back, remove the focus from your situation, and place your focus on others in your life. Find someone in your world who maybe you can create a miracle for, because of God in you. Be the person to deliver it for them. It will radically alter your life.

Taking the leap in life is not just about achieving our dreams and goals. It is about learning that the greatest reward comes from putting others first and having a strong desire to make the world a better place. In the long run, that might be one of the most important leaps we make.

EACH ONE OF US HAS THE POWER TO BE AN ANSWER TO PRAYER IN SOMEONE'S LIFE TODAY.

Research has proven that the best way to achieve happiness is to forget our problems and issues, and serve others. God designed us to love and serve others, and as we do so, we experience true happiness and peace. In fact, in a report in the Proceedings of the National Academy of Sciences, using MRI imaging, subjects' brains were scanned while being asked questions, and they were given a series of tests to perform. Lisa Farino reporting for MSN Healthy Living said, "When participants chose to donate money, the brain's mesolimbic system was activated, the same part of the brain that's activated in response to monetary rewards, sex, and other positive stimuli. Choosing to donate also activated the brain's subgenual area, the part of the brain that produces feel-good chemicals, like oxytocin, that promote social bonding."[1]

There is a scientifically proven benefit for us helping others and being altruistic. However, I believe it is not only good for us physically, but spiritually as well. If we have learned anything since the start of the Great Recession, it is that the world needs more selfless, rather than selfish, people.

Each one of us has the power to be an answer to prayer in someone's life today. Miracles happen, but God often wants to use us to facilitate those miracles here on earth. I am sure I have failed many times when I should have listened to that voice inside urging me to do something. It's easy to make excuses and say I'm consumed with running a business, being a father to five, volunteering on multiple boards and committees, and all the other activities that make up my days. While these things are important, I need to constantly remember to be in prayer and listen for an opportunity to help others. Some of my greatest joys in life have come from helping those in need and seeing how an act of kindness, however seemingly small to me, can mean the world to someone else. It is the most rewarding work we can do. Yes, one person can make a difference in the world. We just have to do it one life at a time.

I believe we live in a world where good people win, good deeds are blessed, and people truly want to help those who have helped them. It not only makes the world a better place but it also makes us happy. Often during this process we will be blessed with new opportunities when we are putting others first and serving to the best of our abilities.

LEAPING BY EXAMPLE

BLESSING OTHERS: Peter Greer, *Hope International, president, bestselling author*

Over a decade before the wheels came off the global economy in 2008, Peter Greer saw the desperate need around the world in developing countries with millions of people unemployed and underemployed. Wanting to work and provide for their families but with no means to do so, Peter saw a way through microfinance to step into this space and give people hope for a better future. Today he is the president of HOPE International, bringing hope to Africa in the form of microfinance loans, which allow people to start their own businesses and become self-sustaining.

When asked about what he has discovered in his work, he stated, "I have come to understand that we are created to give and to be generous. Studies have shown that the pleasure part of the brain is stimulated when we give. It actually makes us happy. They have also shown that our brains receive the same stimulation when giving as a cocaine addict gets when they are high. The Bible says your are more blessed to give than receive and, physiologically speaking, science has proven this to be true." Having witnessed first-hand the poverty in Africa and Southeast Asia, Peter added, "I have seen that the cause of misery around the world is being obsessed with ourselves. Giving allows us to focus on others. When we give, we see ourselves empowered. We start to value our gifts and abilities. When we value ourselves and our abilities, great things happen. Minds are changed and we start to see value in the world, not problems. I think it is important for everyone to give and to be generous no matter where they are in the social-economic spectrum. Generosity is important to live a full and happy life."

Peter went on to say, "There is no shortage of people who need help. It can be right in front of us. We don't have to go to Africa to serve. We all need to start in our own neighborhoods. Start small and simple, and help people around you. Ask yourself, how can I help someone today? Our words of encouragement and support can be the best gift we can give someone. We should start each day being generous with grace and compassion to others in our lives!"

Early in Peter's career when he was applying for a job, the door closed, and he had to "settle" for a position that was not his top choice. "I had no glimmer of hope. I took the job that was a letdown and it ended up being perfect training for me. It helped me launch the next chapter in my life! There are no wasted moments in life. If the door doesn't open for you, learn from your experience, maximize your opportunity, and it will pay off."

STICKING THE LANDING

- Make a list of three people you know that are in need and write an action plan of how you can help each one of them over the next 30 days.

- Get involved with a hands-on service project in your community. This can be through your place of worship or with a national or local organization. Local soup kitchens and Habit for Humanity offer great service projects and are always looking for volunteers.

- For a long-term commitment to help end poverty in your community, go to OpenTable.org to see how you can assist them in their mission. You will be amazed at how you are transformed in the process.

CHAPTER 11

LEAP INTO LEADERSHIP

"Earn your leadership every day." —MICHAEL JORDAN

Over the years I have been asked to speak to young professionals in many settings, from college classrooms to fellowship programs, and I have developed a presentation based on 13 leadership values that I have learned over my career. These come from real-life experience and from the help of mentors along the way.

Taking a leap in life will immediately set you apart from the crowd, as many will not have the courage or strength to lay it all on the line. Those who do are exposed. It can be challenging and scary at times, but it also yields the greatest rewards. When you take the leap—whether by starting your own business or by moving into a greater leadership role within your organization—you will be faced with many new challenges as a leader, and your career and business will often be on the line. Your decisions, your leadership, problem-solving, and how you navigate challenging situations will determine your success or failure. These 13 principles are essential for a leader's success.

1. EVERYTHING RISES AND FALLS ON LEADERSHIP

Author John Maxwell has many quotes but one of my favorites is, "Everything rises and falls on leadership."[1] I have found this to be true in military operations, business launches, and non-profit work around the world. Leadership is key to the success of any organization. One person can make a difference, and no matter where you are or what your title is, you can be a leader and make a difference in the world around you. If others are not leading, stand up and lead through influence to create change. As it has been said many times, leaders must be able to see the invisible if they want to be able to accomplish the impossible.

2. LEADERS CAST VISION

Proverbs 29:18 says, "Where there is no revelation, people cast off restraint; but blessed is the one who heeds wisdom's instruction." All people want to be a part of something greater than themselves. As a leader, get people to see what they can accomplish and help lead them daily in that direction. Everyone wants to be a part of a winning team, and a leader's job is to cast the compelling vision of what victory looks like. Does your vision inspire and bring the best out of those around you?

3. LEADERS MUST BE PRESENT

To lead and accomplish your goals, you must be present. You can delegate tasks to members of your team, but you can't delegate leadership. Today's modern workplace has teams spread out around the world, and many times you will be forced to lead from a distance as you use technology to stay in touch with your team. You may not be physically present, but you must be engaged with situational awareness every day for your team. You need to be mentally engaged at all times, knowing what is going on and the challenges your team is facing. Not so you can micromanage their performance but so that you can effectively lead. A leader's prime job is to inspire and motivate at all times.

Being present each day will also help you use your authority and position to help remove roadblocks and obstacles for the team so they can execute their mission. Many times they will run into issues that at their level they cannot solve, but with one phone call you as the leader can remove obstacles or get needed resources allocated. Organizations that grow fast and win in this environment are ones that move quickly and seize opportunities. This happens with leaders who are constantly engaged and present with everything that is happening.

4. LEADERS LEAD BY EXAMPLE

Poor leaders believe that a leadership position gives them greater rights and privileges. Great leaders understand that they do not have more rights, but because of their leadership position they have more responsibility placed on their shoulders. I witnessed this firsthand in the military as General William Begert, Commander of the Pacific Air Forces, would spend the holidays traveling around Asia meeting the troops and serving them Thanksgiving dinners. He could have stayed home and celebrated the holidays with his family, but the staff knew that we would always be on the road with the General, serving the troops, because he wanted to lead by example. During his tenure as the PACAF Commander he set an amazing example for all the leaders in his chain of command to follow. I once heard a leader say, "If you want your people to bleed for the organization, the leader better be ready to hemorrhage." Never ask your people to do what you are not willing to do yourself.

5. LEADERS ACCEPT RESPONSIBILITY

The "blame game" is a disease of an underperforming organization. Leaders accept responsibility and teach others to do the same. Create a culture where your team knows that accepting responsibility is expected and passing blame on others is not accepted. It is said that Ben Franklin once remarked, "I never knew a man who was good at making excuses that was good at anything else."

Sometimes a leader will be required to accept the mistakes of leaders who went before them and correct them. In my career I have seen how some leaders will throw the previous leader under the proverbial bus and get as much mileage as possible from blaming them even for things they had nothing to do with. There are certainly times when previous leaders make mistakes that need to be corrected. To date, I have never met a perfect leader who never made a poor judgment call. Making mistakes is part of the leadership journey. However, I have also learned to understand that many times past decisions were made with different information or situations. So the decision at the time was the right one, but in the present time it doesn't make sense and needs to be changed. If you are in a leadership position where you have to correct mistakes from the past, take the time to truly understand the environment in which that decision was made. It might be very enlightening and help you with making the right decision in the present.

MAKING MISTAKES IS PART OF THE LEADERSHIP JOURNEY.

6. LEADERS ARE NOT AFRAID TO FAIL

My high school coach taught me early in my running career that I would learn more from my failures than from my successes. I did not realize how insightful that was. This is a recurring message that all great leaders I have studied continue to echo. All things being equal, we all want to win, but we need to change our thinking and realize that many times our failures will give birth to our greatest success. In the start-up world I have heard leaders say, "If you are not failing, you are not trying hard enough." Knowing this, venture capitalists are notorious for telling their early-stage start-ups to "fail early and fail often." It is much cheaper to fail early in a business than to fail later, and they want their young entrepreneurs to test their theories to see if they will work. Mark Zuckerberg, Founder and CEO of Facebook, is credited with saying, "The biggest risk is not taking any."[2] That is a man not afraid of making a mistake. When you have created a culture where people do not fear failure but learn from it and where people accept responsibility, you can start to build a culture of "Kaizen," or continuous improvement. The famous PDCA Deming Cycle of continuous improvement loop (Plan, Do, Check, Act) helps a team make adjustments after every action to continually improve performance. The goal should be to set the example and create a culture where this is hardwired into the DNA of your organization.

7. LEADERS WIN WITH THEIR TEAM

Whether early or late in your career, learning the art of hiring well is crucial. Bad hires are costly. If you make a mistake, fix it quickly. Many HR professionals live by the rule, "Hire slow, fire fast." The wrong employee can do enormous damage to the organization. The opposite is also true as great talent will help the organization grow and will determine the success of your organization. Bill Gates said, "I need people with big bandwidth," and the talent wars in Silicon Valley are legendary as companies work hard to hire away the best and brightest stars of the industry. Bill Gates went on to say, "A great lathe operator commands several times the wage of an average lathe operator, but a great writer of software code is worth 10,000 times the price of an average software writer."[3] The facts are clear that hiring the best talent as you build your team is critical to success.

When building a team, the three most important things are (1) character/integrity, (2) loyalty, and (3) competence. These are especially important in a turn-around environment. If a person does not have good character and integrity, no matter how great they are, they will damage your team in the long run. Your list might be different based on your environment and needs. Remember: "The speed of the leader is the speed of the team." If you are a hard-charger or in a turn-around or high-growth environment, make sure you are hiring a team that can keep up with you and your market!

8. LEADERS CREATE AND PROTECT CULTURE

Every organization has a unique culture that goes deeper than the manuals and written rules and procedures that people follow. Many times the unwritten rules of how an organization thinks and operates have more bearing on the culture than the written mission statements. When building a three-year strategy for an organization, I reached out to an advisor for input and he said, "Bob, remember culture eats strategy for breakfast." His point was that no matter what strategy was developed, the underlying culture of an organization has more to do with its success or failure. As leaders hire, lead by example, take responsibility, and empower their team, they have the ability to create the culture of the organization. Create a culture where the best performers want to come to work and bring their "A-game" and strive to win. To be victorious you need a culture based on integrity, passion for your cause, high energy, and a competitive spirit to be the best you can be at what you do.

9. LEADERSHIP IS NOT A POPULARITY CONTEST

Most everyone likes to be "liked," but as a leader you can't make everyone happy, and you are certain to fail trying to do so. Leaders are paid to make tough decisions and get results. By default, leadership is a polarizing position, and on any given day, someone is going to either be happy or upset with you. Leaders need to have thick skin and be able to live with it. If everyone is happy with a leader, that leader is probably not leading.

IF EVERYONE IS HAPPY WITH A LEADER, THAT LEADER IS PROBABLY NOT LEADING.

Leading requires making changes, and most people are averse to change. As you lead change in an organization, this is where you will step on the most toes and where you will have the potential to anger those who are forced to change and adapt to new marketplace realities. Always treat people with dignity and respect, but never compromise on your leadership or the goals of the organization because some people are unhappy with how it might impact them. Lead on! This requires a delicate balancing act. John Maxwell says if you think you are leading but no one is following, you are just on a long walk.[4] To effectively lead, you have to influence your team to follow your direction to accomplish a goal. My advice is to not allow one or two bad apples in the group to be an obstacle in that effort.

10. YOUNG LEADERS WILL BE CHALLENGED

Early in your career you may be placed in tough leadership positions where people try to take advantage of your youth or inexperience. You will be tested to see if you believe in the direction you are heading and if you have the courage to follow through. Seek advice from mentors and advisors as you make decisions, but trust your gut instincts, be committed, and follow through. Great leaders will lead with compassion as they build their teams, but they must make sure everyone is in alignment with the vision and are willing to follow direction. If someone continually undermines your authority, does not buy into the mission of the organization, and causes problems—no matter how valuable they may be—you must take action and remove them from the team.

11. LEADERS MUST DEAL WITH PROBLEMS QUICKLY AND DIRECTLY

In a crisis, timing is everything. Many leaders are afraid to deal with problems or people head-on and let bad situations get worse by allowing issues to fester behind the scenes. Often organizations die because leaders do not take proper timely action. Time does not make problems go away; it only makes them bigger and more difficult to deal with. Moving fast does not mean making ill-planned decisions based on the moment and an emotion. Great leaders will take in all the information by listening, asking questions, and then discerning the facts. Get outside counsel from mentors who have faced similar challenges and can offer a different perspective. Finally, the leader must *decide* on the course of action and then *act*. Leaders are faced with challenges daily that will require quick decisions based on the internal and external environment. Over time, all leaders grow in this area. No book-knowledge or theory will teach you better than real-world experience.

12. LEADERSHIP SUCCESS RESTS IN FAITH AND FAMILY

In our success-crazed culture, many chase leadership positions for the fame, money, and power that leadership positions often come with. They pursue leadership for all the wrong reasons and many, after a lifetime of success, wake up and realize the things they thought were so valuable are worthless and the things that are truly valuable in life, they lost. I have seen successful leaders who have a trail of broken relationships with friends and family, failing health, and a faith in tatters, wishing they could do it all over. There are no do-overs in life. Money will never buy happiness and the most important things in life will be your faith and family. When the storms of life come they will weather them with you. Your faith will get tested, but that is okay. A faith not tested is a faith that cannot be trusted. When the storms of life come, you will be glad you built your life on a solid foundation!

13. LEADERSHIP COMES WITH A BURDEN MOST WON'T UNDERSTAND

Leadership is a tough and many times lonely position. People who have not been in those positions don't understand the stress and pain that can come with it. Those on the outside see the perks of being a leader but rarely see the negative side of leadership. This has been a challenge leaders through the ages have faced and I am sure it led to the writing of the great fable of Damocles' Sword and the great Roman orator Cicero's telling of it in his fifth disputation.

Over the centuries, the story of Damocles' Sword has been told many ways, but this is how my mentor told it to me, warning me about a life in leadership.

The great King Dionysius, being a loving and caring king, decided to give a banquet to many of his loyal subjects. He gathered everyone in the great dining hall, which offered a stunning view of the kingdom as it stretched out as far as the eye could see. A busy city stretched out below the windows of the great hall and extended past the city walls to the countryside of rolling hills, with majestic mountains in the distance framing this wondrous kingdom full of riches. The guests enjoyed the views and feasted together, appreciating the luxury and splendor of the kingdom. They all marveled at the wealth and great fortune of King Dionysius.

One loyal subject named Damocles approached the throne exclaiming how lucky King Dionysius was to be king and to be able to enjoy all the luxury and wealth his kingdom brought him. King Dionysius pondered that for a moment as he sat on his throne and then asked Damocles if he would like to sit on his throne and see what it was like to be king. Shocked at the amazing offer from the king, Damocles answered without hesitation in a burst of excitement, "Absolutely! I'd love to be king!" So King Dionysius slowly stood and removed his crown and placed it on the head of Damocles. He then stood to the side and gave a smile as he motioned Damocles to sit on the throne and said, "Enjoy!"

Damocles sat there for a moment, taking it all in, while the rest of the banquet hall remained stunned in silence at the developments happening in front of them. Damocles continued to revel in the moment, but the guests noticed something strange. The radiant smile and excitement on Damocles' face quickly turned to sheer terror as he looked to the ceiling. The guests could see nothing except the ornate tapestries that had been brought from all over the world hanging from the ceiling, displaying the majesty of the four corners of the globe. However, unseen to them and only visible to the one sitting on the throne was a great sword, the largest sword ever seen, hanging from the ceiling directly above the throne. This great sword moved ever so slightly with the light breeze in the dining hall, for all that held it in place was a tiny hair of a horse's tail. Damocles jumped up from the throne exclaiming, "King, this is unsafe! At any moment that sword could come crashing down and kill me!" King Dionysius took the crown from Damocles' head, placed it back on his own, and calmly sat back in his throne with a stoic smile on his face, saying, "So it is to be king." Damocles returned to his table, shaken with a new understanding of what others would never know . . . that being king is not always as glorious as it seems.

IF YOU ASPIRE TO LEADERSHIP, MAKE SURE IT IS FOR THE RIGHT REASONS.

As you progress through your career and you make the leap into leadership positions, never make the leap to chase the outward trappings of what those leadership positions offer. The offerings never outweigh the stress and responsibility that comes with it. If you make the leap solely for material gain and the things that those positions offer, you will be very disappointed. Only take a leadership role and position because you care for the people and organization and you want to serve the people and help make the organization better.

Make sure you have the gifting to be successful in that endeavor and you are passionate about the mission and cause. You must have the passion burning deep inside of you, because long after the thrill of success wears off, that is what will motivate you to continue on when many others would have given up.

True success in life lies not in the things we achieve, the awards we win, or the accolades we receive, but in the good we do for others and the world around us. In the end, our faith and family are the things that matter most. Don't ever lose sight of that on your journey as you make the leap in your career. Your faith and family will be with you throughout life and will weather the storms that come your way. We all have seen people who chased success and achieved all the worldly measures of riches and fame but along the way lost their soul, family, and in the end everything they once thought was valuable. Mark 8:36 says, "What does it profit a man to gain the whole world, and forfeit his soul?" (NASB). If you aspire to leadership, make sure it is for the right reasons. You will never understand the mantle of leadership until it is firmly on your shoulders. With this said, all great leaders have to be great followers as well, so in your current role, pray for and help your leaders as much as possible. Understand the burdens they carry, and work to support them. Those who do will be forever in the good graces of the men and women they serve!

Leaping by Example

LEADERSHIP: John Choate, *US Navy SEAL, Defense Venture Group, CEO*

....

Navy SEALs are world-renowned for their tenacity and sheer determination against all odds to accomplish their mission. The leaders of this elite fighting-force are the best of the best. John Choate, graduate of the US Naval Academy, a Navy SEAL, a YPO member, and former CEO of Defense Group, is no exception. As a young leader in the military, he learned that making decisions under intense stress and pressure was critical for mission success. "The better you train, the easier it is to make decisions under stress. You have to be flexible and understand that plans will change all the time," he said.

John also explains the kind of person who will be a good leader in a SEAL unit: "You need to be tactically proficient and understand what your unit can flex to and what the unit can't do. Knowing when to say no is important. You also have to be able to communicate dynamically. Does everyone around you understand the orders and the mission? The leader needs to always provide context for what is going on. Contextualizing the why for your unit is important for mission success."

In dynamic environments, work hard to communicate, and make sure everyone around you understands the "why" for your decisions. In a marriage you would explain to your spouse the reason you would like to cut all discretionary spending and build margin is so that in a year you can launch a business. If they have no context about the future plans, those sacrifices will not be seen as positive. In the end, leadership is not a solo act, but a team endeavor. One person may hold the title of *leader*, but it takes an entire team to execute a successful mission. "I'm a team guy," explained John.

"It always goes back to the team. Teams win, individuals lose. You learn that early on in SEAL training." This holds true in life. As you make plans for your future and your career and you lead teams from your family unit to business units, your ultimate success will be predicated on how you lead yourself and others. Those who are successful always have a great team around them and that can be made up of family, friends, mentors, and advisors. Don't think you have to do this alone. Build your team to aid you in your journey and do the same for others.

STICKING THE LANDING

* Start developing your leadership skills today. Lead where you are and help make a difference in your job and community by volunteering to take on leadership roles and responsibilities that others won't.

* Learn! Read, read, and read some more. This is one of the most important roles as a leader. Learn from the best. I think John Maxwell is one of the best leadership authors and he has many books that cover this topic. I encourage you to read books about other leaders in business and politics to learn how they overcame challenges and led in adversity. Learning from the great leaders of history will help you on your journey.

STICK THE LANDING

"Courage is not simply one of the virtues, but the form of every virtue at the testing point." —C. S. LEWIS

From the beginning of this book, my goal has been to inform you of the economic changes taking place globally so we can better prepare for our careers and retirement. After interviewing economists, CEOs, college professors, business leaders, and people in various stages of their careers all around the globe, I hope I have been able to paint a picture of what I have seen and experienced so you can further investigate and decide what steps you need to take on your journey to have success in this new marketplace. We have covered key areas for personal adjustment in the realm of making proper plans,

LIFE WILL CONTINUE TO GET IN THE WAY IF WE WAIT FOR THE PERFECT TIME TO TAKE STEPS TO CHANGE OUR LIVES.

avoiding anchors, developing our career muscle, diversifying our income, building a personal brand, leveraging social media, getting inside various organizations, and helping others along the way.

Often the most difficult thing to do is to start.

We will all face adversity, and life will continue to get in the way if we wait for the perfect time to take steps to change our lives. As I have highlighted, there is no "perfect time," and the most important thing we can do is to take action. That critical first step moving us toward our goal, even in the face of adversity, is what will give birth to our greatest achievements and success. I hope you have started to formulate a plan in your mind for your future. It could be to reduce your debt and develop your freedom fund. It could be that as you explore what you want your future to be that you start taking action today to live a healthier life and get fit as your first step. I am a firm believer that everyone should have a couple of goals in their life that they are working toward daily. This helps us stay focused, while flexing our internal locus of control, on working hard and taking action. However, taking that first step is just the start. If we do not believe and if we are not fully committed, we will not "stick the landing" and achieve the victory moment we desire. Sticking the landing is the critical last step to achieving our goals because we don't get style points along the way just for starting. We all know people who start but never finish. The world is full of them. Just go to a local gym on January 1 to see a group of "starters." Don't be someone who just "starts"; be someone who "sticks."

The 1996 Olympic Games held in Atlanta, Georgia, had America's attention as superstars like Michael Johnson and Carl Lewis made headlines in track and field, Amy Van Dyken in swimming, Andre Agassi in tennis, and the US women's soccer team winning the gold medal. Even with 10,320 athletes, 271 events, and 26 sports represented, there was one athlete and one moment that became the most memorable of the 1996 games.[1]

The United States had never won the all-around team title in women's gymnastics. The US team in 1996 was led by world-renowned, former Romanian coach, Bela Karolyi. That women's team that entered the competition was considered by many to be the best ever assembled. So good, in fact, they were referred to as the "Magnificent Seven," and the worldwide expectation was they were the clear favorite to win.

Throughout the team competition, the United States and Russia competed against each other as the top two contenders for the gold. After an intense series of events, the United States held a slight lead going into the final stretch. With the United States closing in on victory, all of a sudden, all eyes were turned to the vault as something unusual and unexpected happened: one of Bela's girls fell.

The youngest of the team, Dominique Moceanu, slipped and fell on her first vault, which was something unheard of with Coach Bela Karolyi's athletes. Dominique got up and returned to the starting spot on the runway for her second attempt. She sprinted down the full length of the runway, hit the springboard, and completed her vault, but upon landing slipped and fell yet again. The crowd and the worldwide audience was in shock. With victory at the time seemingly hanging in the balance, the US girls looked to the last vault performer of their team. The responsibility and weight of this moment fell on little Kerri Strug out of Tucson, Arizona.

Kerri took to the runway and leaped into action. Sprinting down the runway toward the springboard and horse, the world watched as the determined gymnast sprang into action, hitting the horse with confidence and maneuvering through the air to her landing, but alas, she under-rotated and immediately fell upon landing. Three falls in a row? It appeared the United States team was unraveling and that the chance of gold might be lost.

To make matters worse, it appeared that Kerri had hurt herself on her first attempt. Limping back to her coach she was heard asking, "Do we need this?" and Bela responded, "Kerri, we need you to go one more time. We need you one more time for the gold. You can do this, you can do it!" The crowd was silent. These were words of confidence and affirmation, a strong voice without fear and stress, speaking life into his athlete and giving birth to victory by his words.

Kerri stood at the end of the runway one last time, staring down at the springboard and horse, the obstacles that she must pass, to stick her landing and secure the gold medal for her team. With a hurt ankle and the world watching, Kerri put any fear out of her mind and tossed aside the pressure of the moment to have intense focus on the challenge before her. She took the first step and then sprinted into action running down the runway, hitting the springboard, and leaping into the air toward her goal. She maneuvered her body like she had thousands of times in practice and "stuck the landing" perfectly, which ushered in a roar from the crowd and the worldwide audience. Her ankle was badly injured and everyone saw it. She picked up her foot ever so slightly, and balancing on one leg, she quickly raised her hands to the air in victory, turned to the judges to salute, and then collapsed on the mat. Her day was done. Her Olympics were done. Her performance is remembered as one of the gutsiest and most memorable performances of any in the modern Olympics. She cried as Bela carried her off the mat, and everyone in the arena cheered for the girl, who against all odds, found the courage to go one more time and leap to the Olympic gold (although it later became clear the US had secured the gold before Kerri's second vault attempt).

The moment you decide to take the leap will be no different. You may not be on an international stage with the eyes of the world upon you, but in your own world you will feel pressure, stress, anxiety, and self-doubt. In your mind you may feel the weight of the world on your shoulders, but like Kerri you need to focus and clear all the external noise from your thoughts as you start to take the first step and execute your plan.

There is one important aspect of Kerri's story that I want you to remember as you embark on your journey. It is easy to miss. There were so many things that must have been going on in that arena, the noise, the shock of the crowd, the pressure building on Kerri, wondering if she could even run down the runway, let alone make a jump and stick the most important landing of her life. With everything going on, Kerri turned to her trusted coach and asked for guidance. In that crucible her coach calmly and with confidence spoke life into her and told her, "You can do it!" He gave her belief, and she ran off and made history! No one is immune from self-doubt. No one is immune from succumbing to the pressure of life and its situations.

I am friends with an Olympic gold-medal winner, a commander of a Navy SEAL unit, several fighter pilots, and award-winning businessmen and women, and although they are all considered the best in their fields, behind the scenes these people have questions of doubt, moments of fear, and feelings of unpreparedness or

> **I HAVE NEVER MET A WINNER IN ANY ENDEAVOR IN LIFE WHO DID NOT HAVE A COACH OR SUPPORT GROUP TO HELP THEM ACHIEVE THEIR GOALS.**

inadequacy. The men and women who I have just mentioned have learned to face their fears and still take that first step. They have learned to overcome their doubts with action. They have learned to seek counsel and mentorship from people they know and trust, who have helped guide them through their career. Like Kerri, they all have coaches and a support group around them. When the storms of life are raging and the pressure builds, those coaches help clear the clutter and silence the noise, externally, and most importantly, internally, by reminding them of their victories in the past and of their hard work and preparation that has brought them to this moment. They remind them they are ready and able to complete the task in front of them. I have never met a winner in any endeavor in life who did not have a coach or support group to help them achieve their goals.

I have been blessed to have some great coaches and mentors in my life from an early age. I learned early in life the value of a great coach, in high school and college athletics. In the military, I learned that teams win over individuals, and we were coached and groomed to handle adverse conditions and situations. In the business world I have sought out those ahead of me to ask for their counsel and guidance on important issues. I have been blessed with great YPO forums where I have been able to confidentially share business and life issues with peers and get feedback and support. One thing I have learned through trial and error is that when I have tried to accomplish a goal alone, my success rate has been much lower than if I have people who help provide coaching, mentorship, and even accountability for me.

For example, as I neared my 40th birthday, I had been trying to get healthier, work out more, and lose some weight. However, I was unable to place my lifestyle changes as a priority over my busy schedule of running an organization and raising five children.

NO MATTER WHAT YOU ARE GOING THROUGH, NO MATTER HOW DIFFICULT IT MAY APPEAR TO BE, YOU CAN CHANGE AND MAKE PROGRESS TOWARDS YOUR GOAL.

Finally, I told two friends I needed them to help hold me accountable to my goal. I drew up a plan of action, and decided to take the leap without looking back. I changed my diet overnight and started working out daily. In three weeks I changed my entire body composition, dropping 16 pounds and increasing my strength and stamina. I feel completely different, and it was due to three things: making a decision, getting accountability partners to help me, and taking daily action toward my goal. My lack of fitness is something that had bothered me for over a year, and within three weeks I was able to take massive steps to resolve it. I had tried to make changes alone with very little success, but when I included others in my journey I made progress.

What is your leap? Maybe you have a big long-term goal like changing jobs or starting a new career. Is your leap starting your own company? Do you want to take a smaller leap by fixing your finances and fully funding your freedom fund? Maybe you want to take the leap with your health. Remember what Anne Beiler said at the end of chapter 5, your pain will give birth to your greatest achievements. It doesn't matter when you start, early or late in life; all that matters is that you take the leap and start today! No matter what you are going through, no matter how difficult it may appear to be, you can change and make progress towards your goal. No one can promise you success, but I can promise you that the process of starting and trying is worth it!

I certainly have set out on a number of goals, done everything to the best of my ability, and fallen short. I have disappointments that elicit deep emotion in me when I think of them even years later. However, I would never trade the journey and my experiences as I worked hard and fought for those goals. They taught me about myself and brought me some of the most amazing experiences I have had in life. I might not have reached certain goals in my life, but I didn't "fail." The experiences I had, the things I learned, and the life I was able to live in the pursuit of those goals is nothing even close to failure. I certainly got a lot further along having tried than if I had never even set out in the first place. I am no longer fearful of failure. I prefer success over the latter for sure, but I enjoy the journey either way. Along the way, I learn, help, encourage, and always try to improve and make progress. You can too! The most important thing I can encourage you to do now is to commit to start.

If you have committed to taking the leap in any area of your life, I recommend that you not do it alone. Start a forum in your local community of two to five people who are all committed to taking the leap with you. Everyone might have different goals, but the accountability of the group will help each of you stay on track with your goals. It is helpful if the people in your forum have similar goals, but it is not necessary. If you have never started a forum like this and would like some help, visit my website, www.RobertDickie .com, to get free forms to download that will help you start and run your forum.

No matter how difficult your leap may seem, no matter how

alone you might feel, no matter how impossible or improbable your goal may seem now, know that the first step in the direction of that goal is one step closer to it becoming a reality. Although your journey, like mine, will be full of twists and turns and with many obstacles to overcome, I trust your faith will grow each day by the action you take and that you will enjoy the journey and learn along the way. I pray that through your actions you will help others and make your community, and the world, a better place. Godspeed!

"In the end, we only regret the chances that we didn't take."
—Unknown

RESOURCES

BOOKS

The World Is Flat by Thomas Friedman
The Founder's Dilemmas by Noam Wasserman
Start Something That Matters by Blake Mycoskie
Free Agent Nation by Daniel Pink
A Whole New Mind by Daniel Pink
Start with Why by Simon Sinek
Career Warfare by David F. D'Alessandro
The 21 Irrefutable Laws of Leadership by John Maxwell
Failing Forward by John Maxwell
The 4-Hour Workweek by Timothy Ferriss
The Speed of Trust by Stephen Covey
What Got You Here Won't Get You There by Marshall Goldsmith
How to Win Friends and Influence People by Dale Carnegie
Outliers by Malcolm Gladwell
The Five Dysfuntions of a Team by Patrick Lencioni
What to Say When You Talk to Your Self by Shad Helmstetter
The True Measure of a Man by Richard Simmons
Business by the Book by Larry Burkett
Living for Jesus by Robert Dickie Jr.
The Root of Riches by Chuck Bentley

WEBSITES/APPS

Mint.com
LearnVest.com
ChristianCreditCounselors.com
GoDaddy.com
HostGator.com
LimeBiscuit.com
LaunchThought.com
WordPress

PayPal
FreshBooks
Square
MailChimp
SendOutCards
Gmail
Google+
Google Drive
Dropbox
Pocket.com
Basecamp
Twitter
Facebook
LinkedIn
YouTube
Instagram
FreeConference.com.
SBA.org
Entrepreneur.com
CareerDirect.org
Crown.org
Crownbiz.com
Newsle
TripIT
TaskRabbit.com
Freelancer.com
Gigwalk.com
Elance.com
Etsy.com
Guru.com
FreelancersUnion.org
Kickstarter.com
Indiegogo.com
GoFundMe.com

PODCASTS

Stanford University's *E-Corner*, "Entrepreneurial Thought Leader" series
Harvard Business Review's *HBR IdeaCast*
Chicago Booth Podcast
London Business School's Official Podcast
Seth Godin's Start-Up School
This Is Your Life with Michael Hyatt
The Andy Stanley Leadership Podcast

CONFERENCES

GiANT Impact Leadercast
Global Leadership Summit
Christian Economic Forum
TED Talks
South by Southwest
Catalyst

EDUCATION

Coursera.org
Codecademy.com
Udacity.com
ReFactorU.com
KhanAcademy.com
CrownBiz.com/venture-academy-listing

NOTES

Chapter 1: A Leap in the Midst of a Black Swan

1. Cheryl K. Chumley, "Cheaper labor: 77 percent of 2013 jobs were part-time positions," *Washington Times*, August 2, 2013. www.washingtontimes.com/news/2013/aug/2/part-timer-nation-77-percent-2013-jobs-were-part-t/.

2. World Economic Forum, "Youth Unemployment Visualization 2013." www.weforum.org/community/global-agenda-councils/youth-unemployment-visualization-2013.

3. Peter Whitehead, "Nearly half of UK workers not on full-time payroll," *Financial Times*, January 29, 2014. www.ft.com/intl/cms/s/0/577bf00e-84f1-11e3-a793-00144feab7de.html#axzz3AhoDmadS.

4. Julie Bort, "Bill Gates: People don't realize how many jobs will soon be replaced by software bots," *Business Insider*, March 13, 2014. www.businessinsider.com/bill-gates-bots-are-taking-away-jobs-2014-3.

5. John Shinal, "Future Economy: Many will lose jobs to computers," *USA TODAY*, March 21, 2014. www.usatoday.com/story/money/columnist/2014/03/21/software-tech-economy-work/6707457/.

Chapter 2: Make a Plan

1. Kelli B. Grant, "Overcoming the $30,000 student loan burden," *CNBC*, May 16, 2014. www.cnbc.com/id/101677274.

2. Pooja Bhatia, "The long-term impact of student-loan debt," *USA TODAY*, March 3, 2013. www.usatoday.com/story/money/personalfinance/2014/03/03/ozy-student-debt/5976111/.

3. Jeanne Beliveau-Dunn, "How the Internet of Everything Is Changing the Game for Tomorrow's Tech Workers," *Huffington Post*, June 5, 2014. www.huffingtonpost.com/jeanne-beliveaudunn/internet-of-everything-tech-workforce_b_5447381.html.

4. Career Direct®, "Research and development technical summary for Career Direct®," 2010. www.careerdirectonline.org/education/R_D.asp.

5. Michael Mandel, "Get it straight: Consumer spending is not 70% of GDP," *Bloomberg Businessweek*, August 29, 2009. www.businessweek.com/the_thread/economicsunbound/archives/2009/08/get_it_straight.html.

CHAPTER 3: AVOID ANCHORS

1. Pooja Bhatia, "The long-term impact of student-loan debt," *USA TODAY*, March 3, 2013. www.usatoday.com/story/money/personalfinance/2014/03/03/ozy-student-debt/5976111/.

2. Board of Governors of the Federal Reserve System, "Consumer Credit Release," August 7, 2014. www.federalreserve.gov/releases/g19/current/default.htm.

3. AP, "$1 trillion student loan debt widens US wealth gap," *CNBC*, March 27, 2014. http://www.cnbc.com/id/101531304.

4. Wikipedia, "The Great Recession," last modified August 13, 2014. http://en.wikipedia.org/wiki/Great_Recession.

5. Juliette Cubanski, Christina Swoope, Anthony Damico, and Tricia Neuman, "Health Care on a Budget: The Financial Burden of Health Spending by Medicare Households," *The Henry J. Kaiser Family Foundation*, January 9, 2014. http://kff.org/medicare/issue-brief/health-care-on-a-budget-the-financial-burden-of-health-spending-by-medicare-households/.

CHAPTER 4: DEVELOP YOUR MUSCLES

1. Jason Selk, "Habit Formation: The 21-Day Myth," *Forbes*, April 15, 2013. www.forbes.com/sites/jasonselk/2013/04/15/habit-formation-the-21-day-myth/.

2. Ibid.

CHAPTER 5: GROW YOUR INCOME

1. Daniel Pink, "Free Agent Nation," *Fast Company*, December 31, 1997. www.fastcompany.com/33851/free-agent-nation.

2. Heidi Shierholz and Lawrence Mishel, "A Decade of Flat Wages," *Economic Policy Institute*, August 21, 2013. www.epi.org/publication/a-decade-of-flat-wages-the-key-barrier-to-shared-prosperity-and-a-rising-middle-class/.

3. Robert Frost, "Mending Wall," 1914. www.poets.org/poetsorg/poem/mending-wall.

4. Walter Isaacson, *Steve Jobs* (New York: Simon & Schuster, 2011), 154.

5. Wikipedia, "Intrapreneurship," last modified June 5, 2014.

6. Annie Jie Xu, "Why All That Planning Is Ruining Your Business—Especially If You're a Woman," *Huffington Post*, August 2, 2013. www.huffingtonpost.com/annie-jie-xu/why-all-that-planning-is-_b_3697191.html#.

7. Project Alopecia, "U.S. Direct Selling Association Announces Annual Sales and Salesforce Figures," August 21, 2014. http://projectalopecia. com/u-s-direct-selling-association-announces-annual-sales-and-sales-force-figures/.

8. Daniel Kaplan, "The Road to $25 Billion," *Sports Business Daily*, January 28, 2013. http://www.sportsbusinessdaily.com/Journal/Issues/2013/01/28/In-Depth/NFL-revenue-streams.aspx.

9. Richard Branson, "Say Yes, Then Learn How to Do It Later," *Virgin. com*, September 18, 2013. www.virgin.com/richard-branson/say-yes-then-learn-how-to-do-it-later.

10. www.freelancer.com.

11. Ignition Event, Speaker Jordan Adler, Las Vegas, NV, February 2014.

12. Sheyna Steiner, "Five Ways to Crash Your Small Business," Bankrate. http://www.bankrate.com/finance/financial-literacy/5-ways-to-crash-your-small-business-4.aspx.

13. Small Business Administration, "What are the major reasons for small business failure?" SBA.gov. http://www.sba.gov/content/what-are-major-reasons-small-business-failure.

14. Susan Kim, "From Spark to Fire: What Turns Ideas Into Opportunities?" *The Business Monthly*, August 2, 2011. www.bizmonthly.com/from-spark-to-fire-what-turns-ideas-into-opportunities/#sthash.Auzdt1ux.dpuf.

15. Eric Ries, "The Lean Startup Methodology," *The Lean Startup*. http://the leanstartup.com/principles.

16. Robin Sharma, "What Richard Branson Told Me About Goal-Getting (And Creating a Life You Adore)," *Huffington Post*, May 15, 2013. www. huffingtonpost.com/robin-sharma/richard-branson-advice_b_3266932. html.

17. Scott Dinsmore, "Simon Sinek Shares the #1 Business Principle that Changes Everything" (video interview), *Live Your Legend*, February 15, 2012. http://liveyourlegend.net/simon-sinek-start-with-why-interview/.

CHAPTER 6: BUILD YOUR BRAND

1. Mary Jesse, "How to Build a Personal Brand," Inc.com, November 27, 2013. www.inc.com/mary-jesse/how-women-leaders-can-build-a-personal-brand.html.

2. Charles R. Swindoll, *Saying It Well* (New York: Hachette Book Group, 2012), Introduction.

3. Michael Synder, "The Real Unemployment Rate: 20% of American Families, Everyone Is Unemployed," *Zero Hedge*, April, 29, 2014. www.zerohedge.com/news/2014-04-29/real-unemployment-rate-20-american-families-everyone-unemployed.

4. Napoleon Hill, *The Law of Success* (New York: Penguin, 2008), 345.

CHAPTER 7: UTILIZE SOCIAL MEDIA

1. Michael Noer, "One Man, One Computer, 10 Million Students: How Khan Academy is Reinventing Education," *Forbes*, November, 19, 2012. www.forbes.com/sites/michaelnoer/2012/11/02/one-man-one-computer-10-million-students-how-khan-academy-is-reinventing-education/.

CHAPTER 8: EXPAND YOUR NETWORK

1. Dennis Nishi, "Take Your Search for a Job Offline," *Wall Street Journal*, March 24, 2013. http://online.wsj.com/news/articles/SB100014241278873 23869604578368733437346820.

CHAPTER 9: JOIN THE TEAM

1. Lauren Weber, "Apprenticeships Help Close the Skills Gap. So Why Are They in Decline?" *Wall Street Journal*, April, 27, 2014. http://online.wsj.com/news/articles/SB10001424052702303978304579473501943642612.

2. Sarah Ayres, "5 Reasons Expanding Apprenticeships Will Benefit Millennials," Center for American Progress, December 2, 2013. www.americanprogress.org/issues/economy/news/2013/12/02/79872/5-reasons-expanding-apprenticeships-will-benefit-millennials/.

3. Nancy Cook, "Should the U.S. Adopt the German Model of Apprenticeships?" *National Journal*, April 11, 2014. www.nationaljournal.com/next-economy/solutions-bank/should-the-u-s-adopt-the-german-model-of-apprenticeships-20140411.

4. Scott Wilson, "Obama announces $600 million in grant programs to prepare workforce jobs," *Washington Post*, April 16, 2014. www.washingtonpost.com/politics/obama-to-announce-600-million-in-grant-programs-to-prepare-workforce-for-jobs/2014/04/16/8feebcb8-c4e9-11e3-bcec-b71ee10e9bc3_story.html.

5. Sarah Ayres, "5 Reasons Expanding Apprenticeships Will Benefit Millennials."

6. Cheryl K. Chumley, "Cheaper labor: 77 percent of 2013 jobs were part-time positions," *Washington Times*, August 2, 2013. www.washingtontimes.com/news/2013/aug/2/part-timer-nation-77-percent-2013-jobs-were-part-t/.

7. European Commission Eurostat, "Employment Statistics," July 2014. http://epp.eurostat.ec.europa.eu/statistics_explained/index.php/Employment_statistics.

CHAPTER 10: PAY IT FORWARD

1. Lisa Farino, "Do Good, Feel Good," *MSN Healthy Living*. http://healthy-living.msn.com/diseases/depression/do-good-feel-good-1.

CHAPTER 11: LEAP INTO LEADERSHIP

1. John Maxwell, "Everything Rises and Falls on Leadership," The John Maxwell Company. www.johnmaxwell.com/about/meet-john/.

2. Leena Rao, "Facebook's Mark Zuckerberg—Insights For Entrepreneurs," *CBS Money Watch*, Oct 31, 2011. www.cbsnews.com/news/facebooks-mark-zuckerberg-insights-for-entrepreneurs/.

3. The New Kingmakers. http://thenewkingmakers.com/.

4. John Maxwell, "Are You Really Leading or Are You Just Taking a Walk?" John Maxwell on Leadership, August 8, 2007. http://johnmaxwellonleadership.com/2012/08/07/are-you-really-leading-or-are-you-just-taking-a-walk/.

CHAPTER 12: STICK THE LANDING

1. Wikipedia, "1996 Summer Olympics." http://en.wikipedia.org/wiki/1996_Summer_Olympics.

ACKNOWLEDGMENTS

"If we never had the courage to take a leap of faith, we'd be cheating God out of a chance to mount us up with wings like eagles and watch us soar." —JEN STEPHENS

First and foremost, I would like to thank God for always being there with wings ready for me during the many times I have blindly leaped into the unknown, this book being one of those many unknowns.

I wish I had enough pages to list all of my teachers, professors, coaches, classmates, and teammates (from Grand Blanc High School, University of Tennessee, University of Arkansas, and Harvard Business School) who have had a profound impact on my life and have each taught me something valuable, showing me how to "develop my muscle" along the way.

My real-life education began during my time in the military, and I am forever grateful to the commanding officers I served under, General William Begert, Colonel Gary Gibbs, Colonel Herman Springer, and to the many others I served alongside who all taught me the importance of the Air Force core values of "integrity first, service before self, and excellence in all you do."

I'm thankful for all the coworkers I have been blessed to work with over the years, especially the team back in Michigan. I learned more from you in those book reviews than most classes I have ever taken. A special thanks goes to Chuck Bentley and my Crown family who have all been supportive and understanding throughout this journey. To my brilliant publicist, Kristi Hamrick, who encouraged me to explore this topic in depth and who has somehow magically made my articles appear in places such as *USA TODAY*, *Fox News*, *The Washington Times*, and other places where they eventually got noticed by the right people. To those "right people," Randall Payleitner and the Moody Publishers team who took a big leap by offering this opportunity to an unknown author. Thank you for allowing me to "join your team." I would be remiss if I didn't mention Bailey Utecht who has helped me "stick the landing" by editing tirelessly. A very heartfelt thank-you goes to two dear friends of mine, Tim Hatmaker who is a constant encourager, and Handre DeJongh who has been a spiritual mentor to me, both friends always giving of their time and "paying it forward" while holding me accountable and keeping me grounded.

And a special thanks to my very first spiritual mentors in life, my parents, Bob and Mary Dickie, who allowed me as a young boy to climb tall trees, and take leaps while getting bumps and bruises, and doctored me up and dusted me off so I could find the next proverbial tree to climb. They were the first to foster courage in me so that I would later be brave enough to take on challenges put in front of me, continually imparting godly advice and valuable wisdom to me along the way.

I'm extremely grateful for my children: my son, Lachlan, who while I thought I was teaching him to have courage, was actually teaching me. Born at four pounds and seven ounces and at one point not expected to make it, Lachlan has always had the heart of a lion and constantly shows me how to push through adversity. My oldest daughter, Trista, who with her tech-savvy ways has taught me most of what I know about social media. #coolestdaughter-ever. She has been a real trooper as my leaps have moved us around often; she has had to change schools and does so with flexibility and resolve. One time she was voted class president after we moved to a new state, and she had only been at her school for one week . . . true story. My little London, who exemplifies tenacity and shows me daily how to overcome obstacles with grit and determination as she never allows her dyslexia to become an "anchor." My Miss Amaris who fills my love tank by the abundance of hugs and kisses she unconditionally gives. She is honestly the most loving child I have ever met, and I'm glad she's mine. And last but not least, my charming Charlize who makes "Papa" feel like a million bucks every time she strokes the side of my face telling me that she loves me. She continually shows me the importance of slowing down and enjoying the simple things of life.

And finally to my beautiful and talented wife, Brandi, who took a major leap in marrying me. She has been a partner in all the leaps we have taken in the military and business world and has been a constant encourager, supporter, and best friend. She has a way of breathing life into me when the trials of life have beaten me down. As the mother to our five wonderful children, she has dedicated her life to building and serving our family and others. I could have never done any of this without her. I look forward to the leaps we will take together in the future.

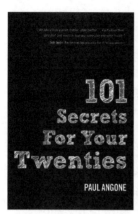

Join our email newsletter list to get resources and encouragement as you build a deeper faith.

Moody Collective brings words of life to a generation seeking deeper faith. We are a part of Moody Publishers, representing this next generation of followers of Christ through books on creativity, travel, the gospel, storytelling, decision making, leadership, and more.

We seek to know, love, and serve the millennial generation with grace and humility. Each of our books is intended to challenge and encourage our readers as they pursue God.

When you sign up for our newsletter, you'll get our emails twice a month. These will include the best of the resources we've seen online, book deals and giveaways, plus behind-the-scenes and extra content from our books and authors. Sign up at *www.moodycollective.com.*

a part of Moody Publishers

From the Word **to Life**

Moody Radio produces and delivers compelling programs filled with biblical insights and creative expressions of faith that help you take the next step in your relationship with Christ.

You can hear Moody Radio on 36 stations and more than 1,500 radio outlets across the U.S. and Canada. Or listen on your smartphone with the Moody Radio app!

www.moodyradio.org